Teach Yourself
VISUALLY™
Photoshop®
Elements 2

by Mike Wooldridge

Visual

From

maranGraphics®

&

WILEY

Wiley Publishing, Inc.

Teach Yourself VISUALLY™ Photoshop® Elements 2

Published by
Wiley Publishing, Inc.
909 Third Avenue
New York, NY 10022
Published simultaneously in Canada

maranGraphics, Inc.
5755 Coopers Avenue
Mississauga, Ontario, Canada
L4Z 1R9

Library of Congress Control Number: 2002114683

ISBN: 0-7645-2515-8

Manufactured in the United States of America

10 9 8 7 6 5 4 3

1K/RY/RS/QS/IN

Trademark Acknowledgments

Important Numbers

For U.S. corporate orders, please call maranGraphics at 800-469-6616 or fax 905-890-9434.

For general information on our other products and services or to obtain technical support please contact our Customer Care Department within the U.S. at 800-762-2974, outside the U.S. at 317-572-3993 or fax 317-572-4002.

Permissions

Ⓦ Wiley Publishing, Inc. is a trademark of Wiley Publishing, Inc.

U.S. Corporate Sales	**U.S. Trade Sales**
Contact maranGraphics at (800) 469-6616 or Fax (905) 890-9434.	Contact Wiley at (800) 762-2974 or fax (317) 572-4002.

Some comments from our readers...

"I have to praise you and your company on the fine products you turn out. I have twelve of the *Teach Yourself VISUALLY* and *Simplified* books in my house. They were instrumental in helping me pass a difficult computer course. Thank you for creating books that are easy to follow."
—*Gordon Justin (Brielle, NJ)*

"I commend your efforts and your success. I teach in an outreach program for the Dr. Eugene Clark Library in Lockhart, TX. Your *Teach Yourself VISUALLY* books are incredible and I use them in my computer classes. All my students love them!"
—*Michele Schalin (Lockhart, TX)*

"Thank you so much for helping people like me learn about computers. The Maran family is just what the doctor ordered. Thank you, thank you, thank you."
—*Carol Moten (New Kensington, PA)*

"I would like to take this time to compliment maranGraphics on creating such great books. Thank you for making it clear. Keep up the good work."
—*Kirk Santoro (Burbank, CA)*

"I write to extend my thanks and appreciation for your books. They are clear, easy to follow, and straight to the point. Keep up the good work!"
—*Seward Kollie (Dakar, Senegal)*

"What fantastic teaching books you have produced! Congratulations to you and your staff. You deserve the Nobel prize in Education in the Software category. Thanks for helping me to understand computers."
—*Bruno Tonon (Melbourne, Australia)*

"Over time, I have bought a number of your 'Read Less-Learn More' books. For me, they are THE way to learn anything easily."
—*José A. Mazón (Cuba, NY)*

"I was introduced to maranGraphics about four years ago and YOU ARE THE GREATEST THING THAT EVER HAPPENED TO INTRODUCTORY COMPUTER BOOKS!"
—*Glenn Nettleton (Huntsville, AL)*

"Compliments To The Chef!! Your books are extraordinary! Or, simply put, Extra-Ordinary, meaning way above the rest! THANK YOU THANK YOU THANK YOU! for creating these."
—*Christine J. Manfrin (Castle Rock, CO)*

"I'm a grandma who was pushed by an 11-year-old grandson to join the computer age. I found myself hopelessly confused and frustrated until I discovered the Visual series. I'm no expert by any means now, but I'm a lot further along than I would have been otherwise. Thank you!"
—*Carol Louthain (Logansport, IN)*

"Thank you, thank you, thank you....for making it so easy for me to break into this high-tech world. I now own four of your books. I recommend them to anyone who is a beginner like myself. Now....if you could just do one for programming VCR's, it would make my day!"
—*Gay O'Donnell (Calgary, Alberta, Canada)*

"You're marvelous! I am greatly in your debt."
—*Patrick Baird (Lacey, WA)*

**maranGraphics is a family-run business
located near Toronto, Canada.**

At **maranGraphics**, we believe in producing great computer books — one book at a time.

maranGraphics has been producing high-technology products for over 25 years, which enables us to offer the computer book community a unique communication process.

Our computer books use an integrated communication process, which is very different from the approach used in other computer books. Each spread is, in essence, a flow chart — the text and screen shots are totally incorporated into the layout of the spread.

Introductory text and helpful tips complete the learning experience.

maranGraphics' approach encourages the left and right sides of the brain to work together — resulting in faster orientation and greater memory retention.

Above all, we are very proud of the handcrafted nature of our books. Our carefully-chosen writers are experts in their fields, and spend countless hours researching and organizing the content for each topic. Our artists rebuild every screen shot to provide the best

clarity possible, making our screen shots the most precise and easiest to read in the industry. We strive for perfection, and believe that the time spent handcrafting each element results in the best computer books money can buy.

Thank you for purchasing this book. We hope you enjoy it!

Sincerely,

Robert Maran
President
maranGraphics
Rob@maran.com

CREDITS

Acquisitions, Editorial, and Media Development

Project Editor
Maureen Spears

Acquisitions Editor
Jen Dorsey

Product Development Manager
Lindsay Sandman

Copy Editor
Jill Mazurczyk

Proof Editor
Technical Editor
Dennis Cohen

Editorial Manager
Rev Mengle

Permissions Editor
Carmen Krikorian

Manufacturing
Allan Conley, Linda Cook,
Paul Gilchrist, Jennifer Guynn

Production

Book Design
maranGraphics®

Layout
Melanie DesJardins,
LeAndra Johnson,
Kristin McMullan

Screen Artists
Jill A. Proll

Illustrators
Ronda David-Burroughs, David E. Gregory

Proofreader
Melissa D. Buddendeck

Quality Control
Laura Albert, David Faust,
Andy Hollandbeck, Charles Spencer

Indexer
Richard T. Evans

Special Help
Mac OS X material provided by Dennis Cohen,
co-author of *Macworld Mac OS X Bible* and
technical editor of this book.

ACKNOWLEDGMENTS

General and Administrative

Wiley Technology Publishing Group: Richard Swadley, Vice President and Executive Group Publisher;
Bob Ipsen, Vice President and Executive Publisher; Barry Pruett, Vice President and Publisher; Joseph Wikert,
Vice President and Publisher; Mary Bednarek, Editorial Director; Mary C. Corder, Editorial Director;
Andy Cummings, Vice President and Publisher.

Wiley Production for Branded Press: Debbie Stailey, Composition Director

ABOUT THE AUTHOR

Mike Wooldridge is a technology writer, Web designer, and educator in the San Francisco Bay Area. He is also the author of several other VISUAL books, including *Teach Yourself Visually Illustrator 10*, *Teach Yourself Visually Photoshop 7*, and *Master Visually Dreamweaver MX and Flash MX*.

AUTHOR'S ACKNOWLEDGMENTS

Many thanks to project editor Maureen Spears for her top-notch editing and guidance. Also, thanks to copy editor Jill Mazurczyk and technical editor Dennis Cohen. It was great working with everyone again.

To Griffin, my three-year-old son,
who loves pressing the buttons
on my digital camera.

TABLE OF CONTENTS

Chapter 1

GETTING STARTED

Chapter 2

UNDERSTANDING PHOTOSHOP ELEMENTS BASICS

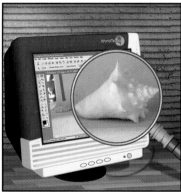

Chapter 3

CHANGING THE SIZE OF AN IMAGE

Chapter 4

MAKING SELECTIONS

Chapter 5

MANIPULATING SELECTIONS

TABLE OF CONTENTS

Chapter 6

PAINTING AND DRAWING WITH COLOR

Chapter 7

ADJUSTING COLORS

Chapter 8

RETOUCHING PHOTOGRAPHS

Chapter 9

WORKING WITH LAYERS

TABLE OF CONTENTS

Chapter 10

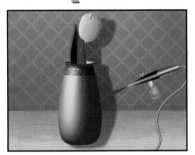

APPLYING EFFECTS AND STYLES

Chapter 11

APPLYING FILTERS

Chapter 12

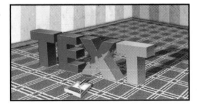

ADDING AND MANIPULATING TYPE

Chapter 13

AUTOMATING YOUR WORK

Chapter 14

SAVING FILES

Chapter 15

PRINTING IMAGES

HOW TO USE THIS BOOK

Teach Yourself VISUALLY Photoshop Elements 2 contains straightforward sections, which you can use to learn the basics of Elements. This book is designed to help a reader receive quick access to any area of question. You can simply look up a subject within the Table of Contents or Index and go immediately to the section of concern. A section is a self-contained unit that walks you through a computer operation step-by-step. With rare exception, all the information you need regarding an area of interest is contained within a section.

The Organization of Each Chapter

Each task contains an introduction, a set of screen shots, and, if the task goes beyond 1 page, a set of tips. The introduction tells why you want to perform the task, the advantages and disadvantages of performing the task, and gives references to other related tasks in the book. The screens, located on the bottom half of each page, show a series of steps that you must complete to perform a given section. The tip portion of each section gives you an opportunity to further understand the task at hand, to learn about other related tasks in other areas of the book, or to apply alternative methods.

A chapter may also contain an illustrated group of pages that gives you background information that you need to understand the sections in a chapter.

The General Organization of This Book

Teach Yourself VISUALLY Photoshop Elements 2 has 15 chapters. Chapter 1 tells you all about the Elements workspace and how to perform essential commands. Chapter 2 discusses selection tools and how to navigate in Elements. Chapter 3 shows you how resize your image. Chapters 4 and 5 tell you how to select a section of an image so that you can manipulate it to suit your needs. You learn the finer points of coloring your image in Chapters 6 and 7. Chapter 8 gives some tips on how to retouch photographs. Chapter 9 illustrates how to place and manipulate your image in layers. You learn about the various effects and filters in Chapters 10 and 11, while Chapter 12 illustrates how to insert type. Chapters 13 through 15 cover how to automate, save, and print out your work.

Who This Book Is For

This book is highly recommended for the visual learner who wants to learn the basics of Elements, and who may or may not have prior experience with a computer.

What You Need To Use This Book

To perform the tasks in this book, you need a computer installed with Photoshop Elements 2 and either OS X (Mac), or Windows XP (PC).

Mac Requirements

- PowerPC® processor: G3, G4, or G4 dual
- Mac OS system software version 9.1, 9.2, or Mac OS X version 10.1 or later
- 128 MB of RAM
- 350 MB of available hard-disk space

Windows Requirements

- Intel® Pentium® II, III, or 4 processor Microsoft® Windows® 98, Windows 98 Special Edition, Windows Millennium Edition, Windows 2000 with Service Pack 2, or Windows XP (recommended upgrade procedure)
- 128 MB of RAM
- 150 MB of available hard-disk space
- For Adobe® PostScript® printers: Adobe PostScript Level 2 or Adobe PostScript 3™

Conventions When Using the Mouse

This book uses the following conventions to describe the actions you perform when using the mouse:

Click

Press and release the left mouse button. You use a click to select an item on the screen.

Double-click

Quickly press and release the left mouse button twice. You double-click to open a document or start a program.

Right-click

Press and release the right mouse button. You use a right-click to display a shortcut menu, a list of commands specifically related to the selected item. If you have a Macintosh with a one-button mouse, you can perform the same operation by pressing `Ctrl` while clicking the mouse button.

Click and Drag, and Release the Mouse

Position the mouse pointer over an item on the screen and then press and hold down the left mouse button. Still holding down the button, move the mouse to where you want to place the item and then release the button. Dragging and dropping makes it easy to move an item to a new location.

The Conventions In This Book

A number of typographic and layout styles have been used throughout *Teach Yourself VISUALLY Photoshop Elements 2* to distinguish different types of information.

Bold

Indicates what you must click in a menu or dialog box.

Italics

Indicates a new term being introduced.

Numbered Steps

Indicate that you must perform these steps in order to successfully perform the task.

Bulleted Steps

Give you alternative methods, explain various options, or present what a program does in response to the numbered steps.

Notes

Give you additional information to help you complete a task. The purpose of a note is three-fold: It can explain special conditions that may occur during the course of the task, warn you of potentially dangerous situations, or refer you to tasks in the same, or a different chapter. References to tasks within the chapter are indicated by the phrase "See the section . . ." followed by the name of the task. References to

other chapters are indicated by "See Chapter . . ." followed by the chapter number. Alternatively, you may find a reference to a specific page number.

Icons

Icons in the steps indicate a button that you must click to perform an operation.

Conventions That Are Assumed With This Book

Window and Mac Conventions

Although this book shows you how to perform steps using a PC, you can also perform them on a Mac. When differences arise between the two operating systems, this book lists the differences in one of two ways:

If a keyboard key or menu option differs, this book lists the PC convention first, followed by the Mac convention in parentheses. For example:

- You can also press `Ctrl` + `A` (`⌘`+`A`) to select all the pixels in an image.

For complicated interface differences, the Mac description often becomes too long or awkward to place in parentheses. Therefore, the PC convention is listed in the numbered step with the Mac convention following it in a bullet:

- Click ⬇ and select a folder in which to save the file.

- On a Mac, click ⬆ and then the column view to locate a folder in which to save the file.

In addition, the bulleted steps that contain results also list both platforms:

- In Windows, the Browse for Folders dialog box appears. On a Mac, the Choose a batch folder dialog box appears.

Operating Differences between OS Versions

This book assumes that, if you are using a Mac, you have OS X installed on your computer. Other OS versions may give different results than those presented in this book.

Getting Started

Are you interested in creating, modifying, combining, and optimizing digital images on your computer? This chapter introduces you to Adobe Photoshop Elements, a popular software application for working with digital images.

WORKING WITH IMAGES

Photoshop Elements lets you create, modify, combine, and optimize digital images. You can then save the images to print out or use online.

Manipulate Photos

As its name suggests, Photoshop Elements excels at editing digital photographs. You can use the program to make subtle changes, such as to adjust the color in a scanned photo, or you can use its elaborate filters to make your snapshots look like abstract art. See Chapter 7 for more about adjusting color and Chapter 11 for more about filters.

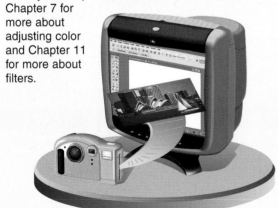

Paint Pictures

Photoshop Elements' painting features make it a formidable illustration tool as well as a photo editor. You can apply colors or patterns to your images with a variety of brush styles. See Chapter 6 for more about applying color. In addition, you can use the application's typographic tools to integrate stylized letters and words into your images. See Chapter 12 for more about type.

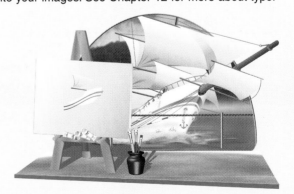

Create a Digital Collage

You can combine different image elements in Photoshop Elements. Your compositions can include photos, scanned art, text, and anything else you can save on your computer as a digital image. By placing elements in Elements onto separate layers, you can move, transform, and customize them independently of one another. See Chapter 9 for more about layers.

Organize Your Photos

Photoshop Elements offers useful ways to keep your images organized after you edit them. You can archive your images on contact sheets or display them in a Web photo gallery. You can even send your images to someone else with the Attach to E-mail feature. See Chapter 13 for more information.

Put Your Images to Work

After you edit your work, you can utilize your images in a variety of ways. Photoshop Elements lets you print your images, save them in a format suitable for placement on a Web page, or prepare them for use in a page-layout program. See Chapter 15 for more about printing. See Chapter 14 for more about using images on the Web.

UNDERSTANDING PHOTOSHOP ELEMENTS

**Photoshop Elements'
tools let you move, color,
stylize, and add text to
your images. You can
correct color flaws in
your photographs or turn
them into interesting
works of art.**

Understanding Pixels

Digital images in Photoshop Elements consist of tiny,
solid-color squares called *pixels*. Photoshop Elements
works its magic by rearranging and recoloring these
squares. If you zoom in close, you can see the pixels
that make up your image. For more on the Zoom tool,
see Chapter 2.

Choose Your Pixels

To edit specific pixels in your image, you first have to
select them by using one of Photoshop Elements'
selection tools. See Chapter 4 for more on selection tools.
Photoshop Elements also has a number of commands
that help you select specific parts of your image, including
commands that expand or contract your existing selection
or select pixels of a specific
color. Chapter 5 covers these
commands.

Paint

After selecting your pixels, you can apply color to them by using Photoshop Elements' paintbrush, airbrush, and pencil tools. You can also fill your selections with solid or semitransparent colors. Painting is covered in Chapter 6.

Adjust Color

You can brighten, darken, and change the hue of colors in parts of your image with Photoshop Elements' Dodge, Burn, and similar tools. Other commands display interactive dialog boxes that let you make wholesale color adjustments, letting you precisely correct overly dark or light digital photographs. See Chapter 7 for details.

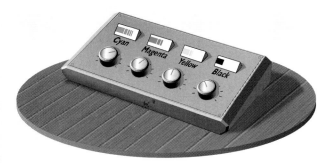

Apply Effects and Filters

Photoshop Elements' effects let you easily add drop shadows, frame borders, and other styles to your images. You can also perform complex color manipulations or distortions by using Photoshop filters. Filters can make your image look like an impressionist painting, apply sharpening or blurring, or distort your image in various ways. Chapters 10 and 11 cover effects and filters.

Add Type

Photoshop Elements' type tools enable you to easily apply titles and labels to your images. You can combine these tools with the application's special effects commands to create warped, 3-D, or wildly colored type. You can find out more about type in Chapter 12.

You can start Photoshop Elements on a PC and begin creating and editing digital images.

START PHOTOSHOP ELEMENTS ON A PC

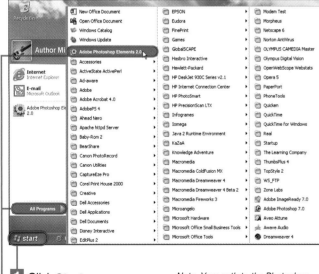

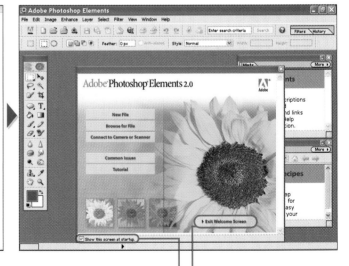

1 Click **Start**.

2 Click **All Programs**.

3 Click **Adobe Photoshop Elements**.

Note: Your path to the Photoshop Elements application may differ depending on how you installed your software.

■ Photoshop Elements starts.

■ A window appears with clickable shortcuts to common Elements tasks.

■ You can click **Exit Welcome Screen** to close the window.

■ You can click **Show this screen at startup** (☑ changes to ☐) to avoid the window in the future.

You can start Photoshop
Elements on a Macintosh
and begin creating and
editing digital images.

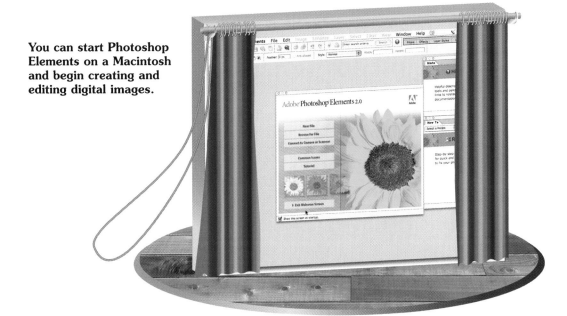

START PHOTOSHOP ELEMENTS ON A MAC

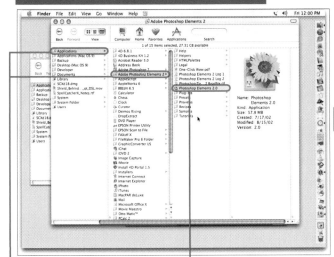

1 Click the Finder icon
( ) in the Dock.

2 Click the Applications
icon ( ) in the Finder
window's toolbar.

3 Double-click the Adobe
Photoshop Elements 2
folder icon ( ).

4 Double-click the
Photoshop Elements 2.0
icon ( ).

*Note: The exact location of the
Adobe Photoshop Elements icon
may be different, depending on how
you installed your software and what
Mac OS version you have.*

■ Photoshop Elements
starts.

■ A window appears with
clickable shortcuts to
common Elements tasks.

■ You can click **Exit
Welcome Screen** to
close the window.

■ You can click **Show
this screen at startup**
(changes to) to avoid
the window in the future.

THE PHOTOSHOP ELEMENTS PC WORKSPACE

You can use a combination of tools, menu commands, and palette-based features to open and edit your digital images in Photoshop Elements on a PC. For more information about palettes, see the section "Open or Close Palettes."

Shortcuts Bar

Displays clickable icons for common commands and a search form for getting help.

Options Bar

Displays controls that let you customize the selected tool in the toolbox.

Elements Toolbox

Displays a variety of icons, each one representing an image-editing tool. You click and drag inside your image to apply most of the tools.

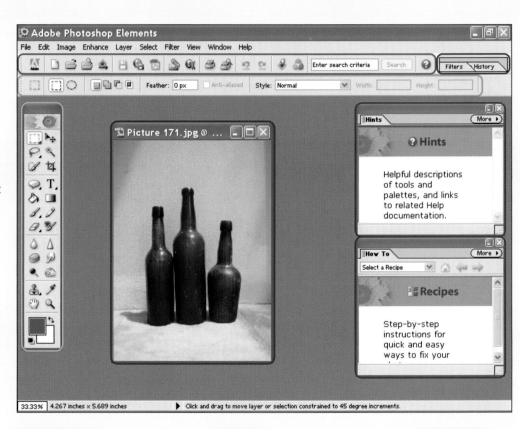

Image Window

Contains each image you open in Elements.

Palettes

Small, free-floating windows that give you access to common commands and resources.

Palette Well

Stores palettes not currently in use.

You can use a combination of tools, menu commands, and palette-based features to open and edit your digital images in Photoshop Elements on a Mac. For more information about palettes, see the section "Open or Close Palettes."

Shortcuts Bar

Displays clickable icons for common commands and a search form for getting help.

Options Bar

Displays controls that let you customize the selected tool in the toolbox.

Elements Toolbox

Displays a variety of icons, each one representing an image-editing tool. You click and drag inside your image to apply most of the tools.

Image Window

Contains each image you open in Elements.

Palettes

Small, free-floating windows that give you access to common commands and resources.

Palette Well

Stores palettes not currently in use.

FIND IMAGES FOR YOUR PROJECTS

You can get raw material for using Photoshop Elements from a variety of sources.

Start from Scratch

You can create your Photoshop Elements image from scratch by opening a blank canvas in the image window. Then you can apply color and patterns with Photoshop's painting tools or cut and paste parts of other images to create a composite. See the section "Create a New Image" in this chapter for more on opening a blank canvas.

Scanned Photos and Art

A scanner gives you an inexpensive way to convert existing paper-based content into digital form. You can scan photos and art into your computer, retouch and stylize them in Photoshop Elements, and then output them to a color printer.

Clip Art

If you want a wide variety of image content to work with, consider buying a clip art collection. Such collections usually include illustrations, photos, and decorative icons that you can use in imaging projects. Most software stores sell clip art; you can also buy downloadable clip art online.

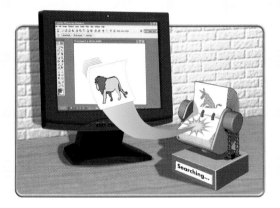

Digital Photos

Digital cameras are a great way to get digital images onto your computer. Most digital cameras save their images in JPEG or TIFF format, both of which you can open and edit in Photoshop Elements. The program's color adjustment tools are great for correcting color and exposure flaws in digital camera images.

Web Images

If you have photos or art stored on the Web, you can easily save those image files to your computer and then open them up in Photoshop Elements. In Microsoft Internet Explorer on the PC, you can save a Web image by right-clicking it and selecting the **Save Picture As** command. In Microsoft Internet Explorer on the Mac, you can option-click an image and select **Download Image to Disk**.

Sample Images

Photoshop Elements comes with several example images that you can open and experiment with. They are useful if you have nothing else to work with and want to get started right away. You can find the images inside the Photoshop Elements application folder in a subfolder called Samples.

OPEN OR CLOSE PALETTES

You can open free-floating windows called *palettes* to access different Elements features. Elements stores closed palettes in the palette well.

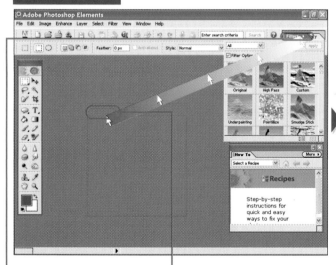

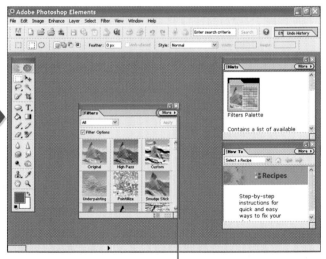

1 Click a tab in the palette well.

■ The palette opens.

■ You can also click **Window** and then a palette name to open a palette.

2 Click and drag the tab to the work area.

3 Release the mouse.

■ The palette opens as a free-floating window.

■ You can click the **More** button to access commands relevant to the palette.

How do I enlarge the palette well?

The width of the palette well depends on the screen resolution of your computer monitor. You can enlarge the well by increasing the resolution. The palette well is narrow and difficult to use at resolutions of 800 by 600 and lower.

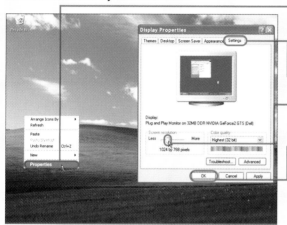

1 On a PC, right-click your desktop and select **Properties** from the menu that appears.

■ The Display Properties dialog box opens.

2 Click the **Settings** tab.

3 Click and drag the Screen resolution slider ( ) to the right to increase the resolution.

4 Click **OK**.

■ On a Mac, click the monitor icon in the menu bar and click a resolution.

■ The screen resolution changes.

CLOSE PALETTES

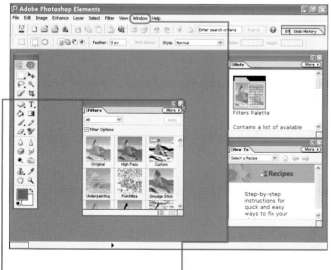

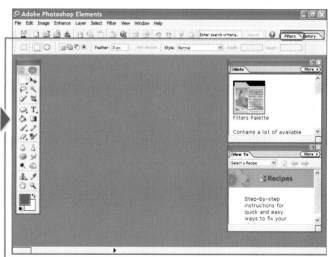

1 Click the Close button ☒ ( ).

■ You can also click **Window** and then a palette name to close a palette.

■ The palette closes and its tab appears in the palette well.

SET PREFERENCES

Photoshop Elements'
Preferences dialog
boxes let you change
default settings and
customize how the
program looks.

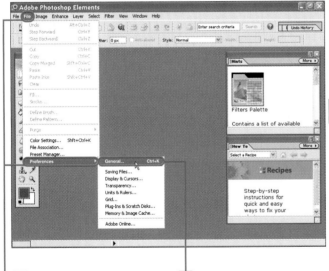

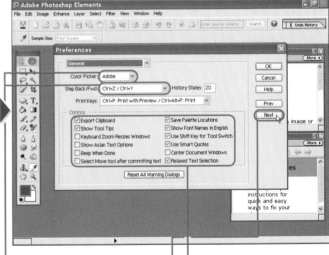

1 Click **Edit**.

■ For a Mac, click the
Photoshop Elements
menu.

2 Click **Preferences**.

3 Click **General**.

■ The Preference dialog
box appears and displays
General options.

4 Click here to determine
which dialog box appears
when you select a color.

5 Click here to select
a keyboard shortcut for
stepping through recent
commands.

6 Click the interface
options you want to use
(☐ changes to ☑).

7 Click **Next** to go to the
Saving Files options.

How do I set the default measurement units for Elements?

You can set the default measurement units for Elements under the **Units & Rulers** options in the Preferences dialog box. These options allow you to specify what units appear by default when you resize an image. See Chapter 3 for more information on resizing images. You can also specify the units that appear on window rulers. See Chapter 2 for how to turn on rulers.

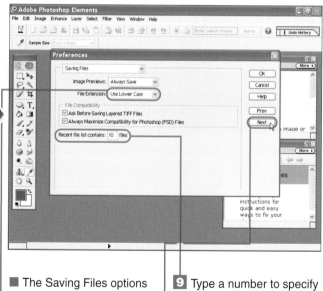

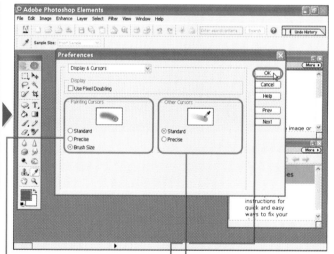

■ The Saving Files options appear.

8 Click here to determine the default file extension case.

■ For a Mac, you can click **Use Lower Case** (☐ changes to ☑) and the desired option in the Image Previews box.

9 Type a number to specify how many recent files are listed under the File menu.

10 Click **Next** to go to the Display & Cursors screen.

■ The Display & Cursors options appear.

11 Click a cursor type to use for the painting tools — the paintbrush, eraser, and others (◯ changes to ◉).

12 Click a cursor type to use for the other tools (◯ changes to ◉).

13 Click **OK**.

■ Elements sets preferences to your specifications.

GET HELP

Photoshop Elements comes with plenty of electronic documentation that you can access in case you ever need help.

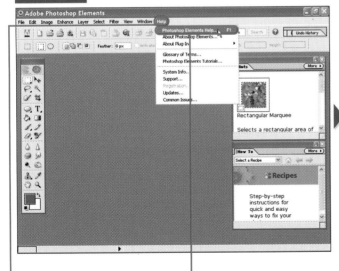

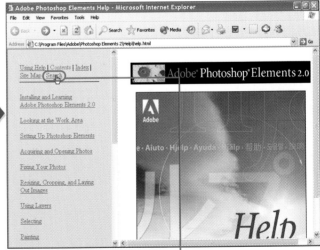

1 Click **Help**.

2 Click **Photoshop Elements Help**.

■ Elements opens a Web browser and displays the Help documentation.

3 Click **Search** to search for information about a particular topic.

Is there a shortcut for looking up help topics?

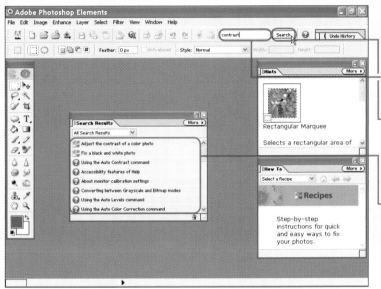

1 Type a help topic in the search box in the Shortcuts bar.

2 Click **Search**.

■ Elements displays results of the search in the Search Results panel.

■ You can click an item in the panel to view more information.

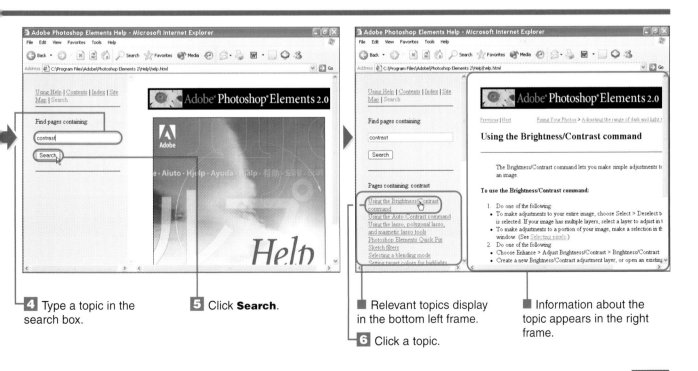

4 Type a topic in the search box.

5 Click **Search**.

■ Relevant topics display in the bottom left frame.

6 Click a topic.

■ Information about the topic appears in the right frame.

The Hints palette briefly explains how to use the currently selected tool or palette. Hints are useful if you want to quickly know how a feature in Elements works.

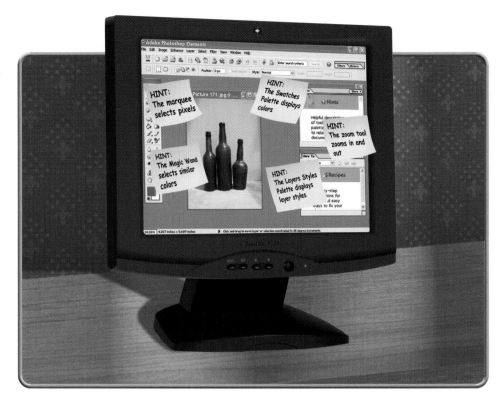

VIEW HINTS

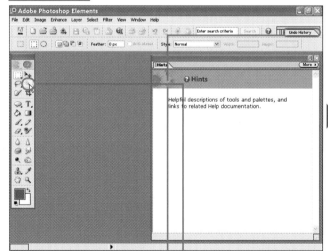

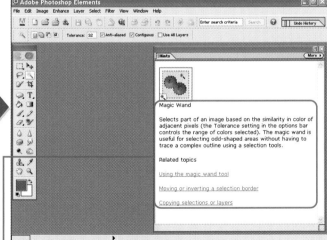

1 Open the Hints palette.

Note: See the section "Open or Close Palettes" for more information.

2 Place your cursor (⟍) over a tool in the toolbox.

■ You can view hints about a palette by placing your cursor over a tab in the palette well.

■ Information about the tool displays.

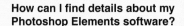

**How can I find details about my
Photoshop Elements software?**

Help

Photoshop Elements Help...	F1
About Photoshop Elements...	
About Plug-In	►
Glossary of Terms...	
Photoshop Elements Tutorials...	
System Info...	
Support...	
Registration...	
Updates...	
Common Issues...	

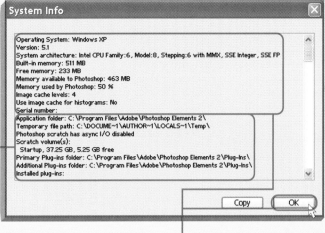

System Info

Operating System: Windows XP
Version: 5.1
System architecture: Intel CPU Family:6, Model:8, Stepping:6 with MMX, SSE Integer, SSE FP
Built-in memory: 511 MB
Free memory: 233 MB
Memory available to Photoshop: 463 MB
Memory used by Photoshop: 50 %
Image cache levels: 4
Use image cache for histograms: No
Serial number:
Application folder: C:\Program Files\Adobe\Photoshop Elements 2\
Temporary file path: C:\DOCUME~1\AUTHOR~1\LOCALS~1\Temp\
Photoshop scratch has async I/O disabled
Scratch volume(s):
  Startup, 37.25 GB, 5.25 GB free
Primary Plug-ins folder: C:\Program Files\Adobe\Photoshop Elements 2\Plug-Ins\
Additional Plug-ins folder: C:\Program Files\Adobe\Photoshop Elements 2\Plug-Ins\
Installed plug-ins:

Copy   OK

1 Click **Help**.

2 Click **System Info**.

■ A window opens displaying
information about your Elements
software, including where it is
installed and what plug-ins
you have available.

■ It also lists basic information
about your computer's operating
system and memory.

3 Click **OK** to exit the window.

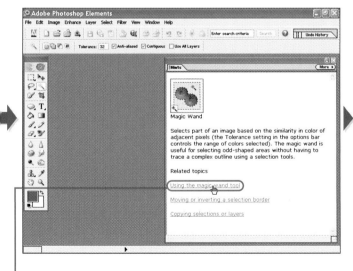

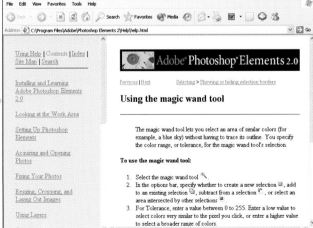

3 To view more detailed
information, click a related
topic hyperlink in the Hints
palette.

■ Information from the
Elements help documentation
displays in a browser window.

*Note: For more information about
Elements help, see the section
"Get Help."*

USING A HOW-TO RECIPE

The How To palette displays step-by-step recipes for performing common image-editing tasks. The recipes can help you become accustomed to using Photoshop Elements.

USING A HOW-TO RECIPE

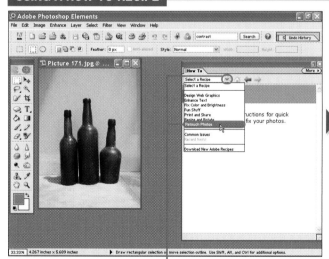 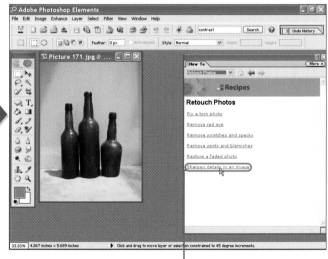

1 Open the How To palette.

Note: See the section "Open or Close Palettes" for more information.

2 Click ().

3 Click a recipe category.

■ A listing of topics for that category displays.

4 Click a recipe topic.

Are there recipes for correcting color problems or flaws in my digital photos?

Photoshop Elements includes a number of recipes for fixing digital photos. Open the How To palette and then select the **Fix Color and Brightness** or **Retouch Photos** categories to access these recipes. Some of the topics include removing a color cast and getting rid of scratches and specks.

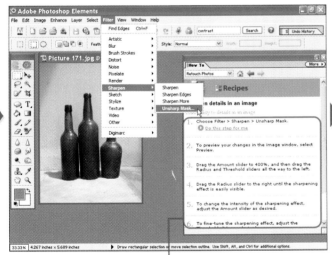

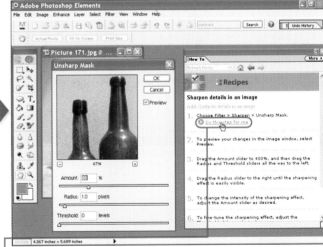

■ The How To palette displays the steps required to complete the topic.

5 Complete each step in the recipe.

■ In the example above, the first step in the recipe is performed.

6 Click ● or the **Do this step for me** link to have Elements automatically complete a step.

■ Elements completes the step for you.

■ In this example, Elements opens the Unsharp Mask dialog box.

OPEN AN IMAGE

You can open an existing image file in Photoshop Elements to modify it or use it in a project.

OPEN AN IMAGE

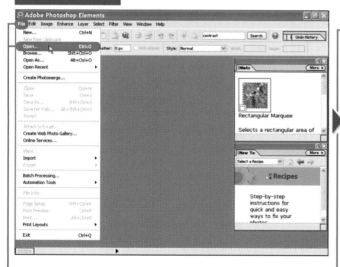

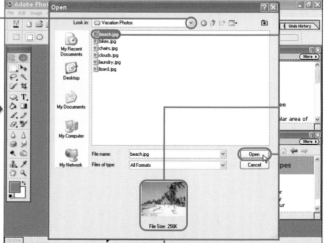

OPEN AN EXISTING IMAGE

1 Click **File**.

2 Click **Open**.

■ You can also click the Folder icon (🗁) in the Shortcuts bar to open the file.

■ The Open dialog box appears.

3 Click ⊻ to browse to the folder that contains the image you want to open.

■ On a Mac, click 🛟 in the From box to browse a folder.

4 Click the filename of the image you want to open.

■ A preview of the image displays.

5 Click **Open**.

What types of files can Photoshop Elements open?

Photoshop Elements can open most of the image file formats in common use today, including:

BMP (Bitmap)	The standard Windows image format
EPS (Encapsulated PostScript)	A popular format for print on Windows and Macintosh.
GIF (Graphics Interchange Format)	A format for Web images
JPEG (Joint Photographic Experts Group)	Another format for Web images
PDF	The image format standard for Macintosh's OS X
PICT	The image format standard for Macintosh's OS9
PSD (Photoshop Document)	Photoshop's native file format
TIFF (Tagged Image Format)	Another print-oriented format.

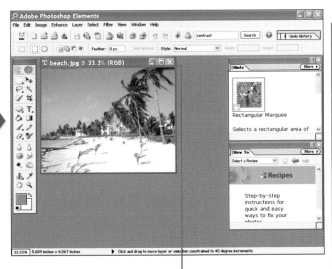

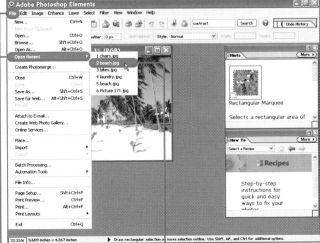

■ Elements opens the image in a new window.

■ The filename appears in the title bar.

OPEN RECENTLY ACCESSED IMAGES

-**1** Click **File**.

-**2** Click **Open Recent**.

■ A list of recently opened files displays.

Note: To specify the number of files that appear in the menu, see the section "Set Preferences."

-**3** Click the image's filename.

■ Elements opens the image in a new window.

BROWSE FOR AN IMAGE

You can open an existing
image file by using
Photoshop Elements'
File Browser.
Browsing offers a
user-friendly way
to find and open
your images.

BROWSE FOR AN IMAGE

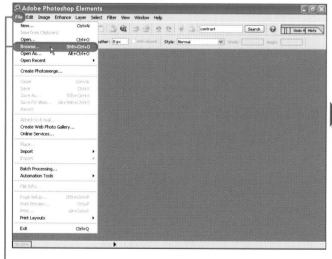

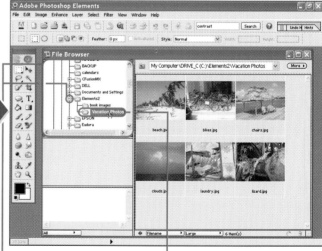

1 Click **File**.

2 Click **Browse**.

■ You can also open the
File Browser as you would a
palette. Click **Window** and
then **File Browser**.

■ The File Browser opens.

■ The folders of your
computer's file system
display.

3 Click ⊞ to open a folder
(⊞ changes to ⊟).

■ On a Mac, click ▶
(▶ changes to ▼).

4 Click a folder.

Where should I store my images on my computer?

You may find it helpful to keep all of your images in one place somewhere central on your computer, such as on your desktop or inside your My Documents folder if you have Windows. For a Mac, you can place images in either your Documents folder or Pictures folder. You may want to create subfolders named with dates or subjects to further organize the images. Keeping images in one place makes it easy to access them from Photoshop Elements.

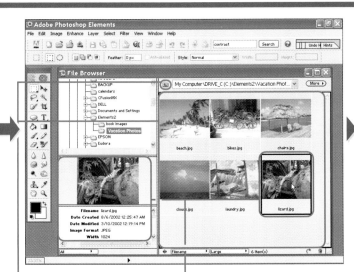

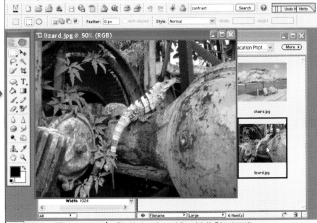

■ The image contents of the folder display.

■ You can click [icon] to move up a level in the folder hierarchy.

■ You can click an image file to view information about it.

5 Double-click an image file to open it.

■ The image opens.

CREATE A NEW IMAGE

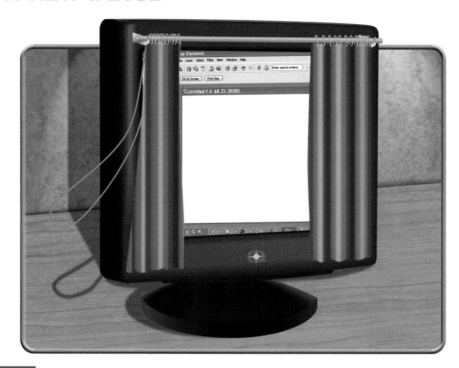

You can start a Photoshop Elements project by creating a blank image.

CREATE A NEW IMAGE

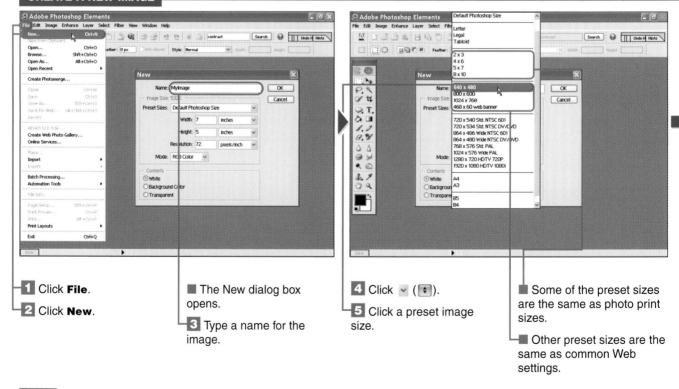

1 Click **File**.

2 Click **New**.

■ The New dialog box opens.

3 Type a name for the image.

4 Click ⌄ (⬍).

5 Click a preset image size.

■ Some of the preset sizes are the same as photo print sizes.

■ Other preset sizes are the same as common Web settings.

How do I choose a resolution for a new image?

The appropriate resolution depends on how you will eventually use the image. For Web or multimedia images, select 72 pixels/inch — the standard resolution for on-screen images. To print black-and-white images on regular paper on a laser printer, 150 pixels/inch probably suffices. For full-color magazine or brochure images, you should use a higher resolution — at least 250 pixels/inch.

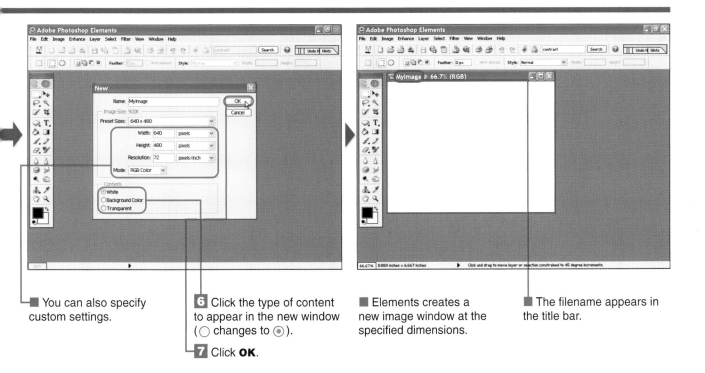

■ You can also specify custom settings.

6 Click the type of content to appear in the new window (○ changes to ◉).

7 Click **OK**.

■ Elements creates a new image window at the specified dimensions.

■ The filename appears in the title bar.

SAVE AN IMAGE

You can save an image in Photoshop Elements to store any changes that you make to it.

Consider saving your images regularly to avoid losing important changes in the event of a system crash.

SAVE AN IMAGE

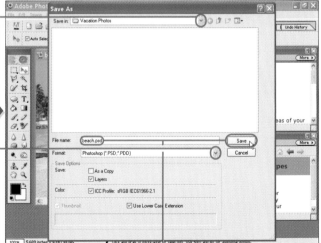

1 Click **File**.

2 Click **Save As**.

■ The Save As dialog box appears.

Note: For images that you have previously saved, you can simply click File and then Save.

3 Click ⌄ to select a folder to store the file.

■ On a Mac, click ⬦ in the Where box.

4 Click ⌄ (⬦) to select a file format.

Note: See Chapter 14 for more information on formats.

5 Type a name for the file. On a Mac, type in the Save box.

6 Click **Save**.

■ Elements saves the image file.

You can exit Photoshop Elements after you finish using the application.

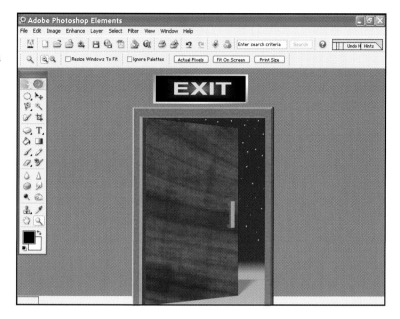

You should always exit Elements and all other applications before shutting down your computer.

EXIT PHOTOSHOP ELEMENTS

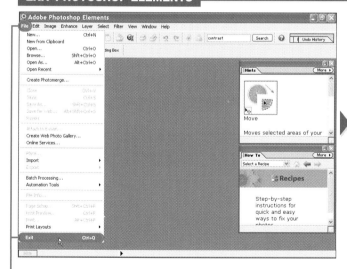

1 Click **File**.

2 Click **Exit**.

■ For a Mac, click **Photoshop Elements** and then click **Quit**.

3 Elements exits.

■ Before exiting, Elements alerts you to any open images that have unsaved changes so you can save them.

Note: See the section "Save an Image" to save image files.

CHAPTER 2

Understanding Photoshop Elements Basics

Are you ready to start working with images? This chapter shows you how to select tools and fine-tune your workspace.

Undo History

Open File
Rectangle Marquee
Deselect
Rectangle Marquee
Paint Bucket
Airbrush
Magic Wand

MAGNIFY WITH THE ZOOM TOOL

You can change the magnification of an image with the Zoom tool. This allows you to view small details in an image or view an image at full size.

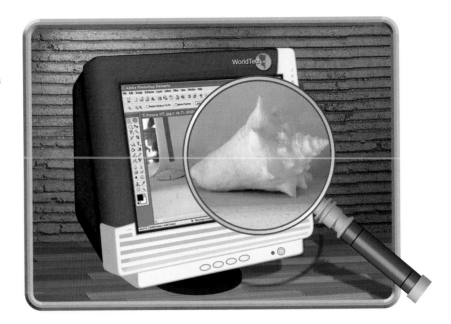

MAGNIFY WITH THE ZOOM TOOL

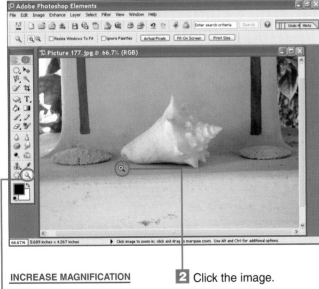

INCREASE MAGNIFICATION

1 Click the Zoom tool ().

2 Click the image.

■ Elements increases the magnification of the image.

■ The current magnification shows in the title bar and status bar.

■ You can choose an exact magnification by typing a percentage value in the status bar.

34

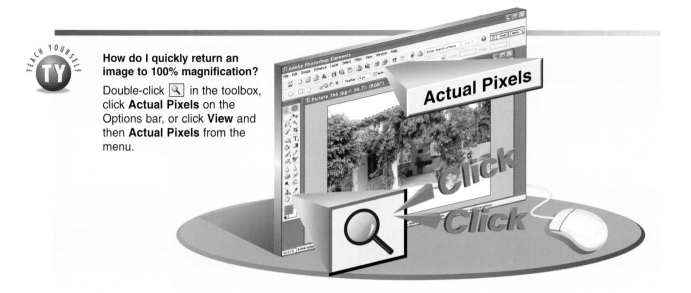

How do I quickly return an image to 100% magnification?

Double-click 🔍 in the toolbox, click **Actual Pixels** on the Options bar, or click **View** and then **Actual Pixels** from the menu.

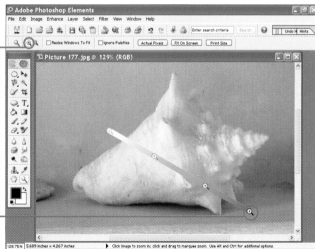

DECREASE MAGNIFICATION

1 Click the Zoom Out button (🔍).

2 Click the image.

■ Elements decreases the magnification of the image.

Note: You can also press and hold **Alt** *and click the image to decrease magnification.*

MAGNIFY A DETAIL

1 Click the Zoom In button (🔍).

2 Click and drag with the Zoom tool to select the detail.

3 Release the mouse button.

■ The object appears enlarged on-screen.

ADJUST VIEWS

You can move an image within the window by using the Hand tool or scroll bars. The Hand tool helps you navigate to an exact area on the image.

The Hand tool is a more flexible alternative to using the scroll bars because, unlike the scroll bars, the Hand tool enables you to drag the image freely in two dimensions.

ADJUST VIEWS

USING THE HAND TOOL

1 Click the Hand tool (✋).

Note: For ✋ to produce an effect, the image must be larger than the image window.

2 Click and drag inside the image window.

36

How can I quickly adjust the image window to see the entire image at its largest possible magnification on-screen?

You have three different ways to magnify the image to its largest possible size: By double-clicking , by clicking the **Fit On Screen** button on the Options bar, or by clicking **View** and then **Fit on Screen** from the menu. Elements adjusts the size of the image so that any open palettes do not overlap it.

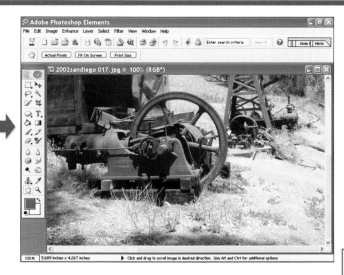

■ The view of the image shifts inside the window.

USING THE SCROLL BARS

1 Click and hold the window's horizontal scroll bar button (◄).

■ The image scrolls horizontally.

VIEW RULERS

You can turn on rulers to help you accurately measure and place objects in your image. Rulers let you place objects a specific distance from one another.

You can turn on a grid to place objects with even more precision. See the section "View a Grid" for more information.

VIEW RULERS

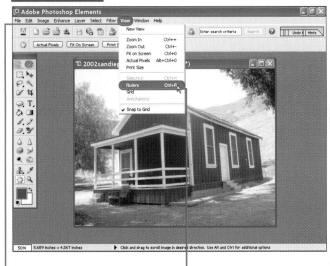

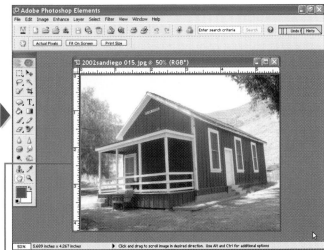

1 Click **View**.

2 Click **Rulers**.

■ Photoshop adds rulers to the top and left sides of the image window.

■ To adjust the units of the rulers, click **Edit** (**Photoshop Elements**), **Preferences**, and then **Units & Rulers**.

You can turn on a grid that overlays your image. A grid can help you precisely organize objects within your image, especially when you have the rulers turned on.

See the section "View Rulers" in this chapter for more on rulers.

VIEW A GRID

1 Click **View**.

2 Click **Grid**.

■ A grid appears on top of the image.

■ To adjust the space separating the grid lines, click **Edit** (**Photoshop Elements**), **Preferences**, and then **Grid**.

■ When you select **View** and then **Snap to Grid**, objects in an image align with the grid lines when you move the objects close to them.

USING SHORTCUTS TO SELECT TOOLS

You can press letter keys to select items in the toolbox. You may find this more efficient than clicking on the tools.

Each tool in the toolbox has a letter associated with it. Elements allows you to easily determine this letter.

USING SHORTCUTS TO SELECT TOOLS

1 Place the cursor ([cursor icon]) over a tool in the toolbox and hold it there.

■ A small box appears that describes the tool and gives its shortcut key.

2 Press the indicated letter to select the tool.

■ Elements automatically selects the tool icon in the toolbox and [cursor] becomes the new tool.

Note: You can modify the shape of the cursor by adjusting Photoshop's Preferences settings. See Chapter 1 for more information.

■ You can use the following shortcut keys to activate common Photoshop tools:

M Marquee **V** Move
L Lasso   **B** Paintbrush
T Type   **Z** Zoom

USING THE SHORTCUTS BAR

You can click buttons on the Shortcuts bar to avoid having to go to the menus to execute commands.

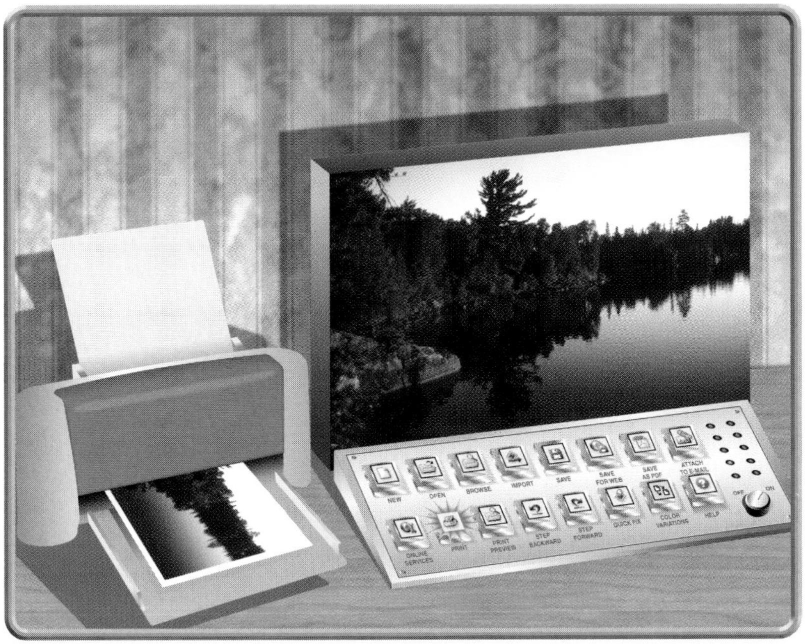

USING THE SHORTCUTS BAR

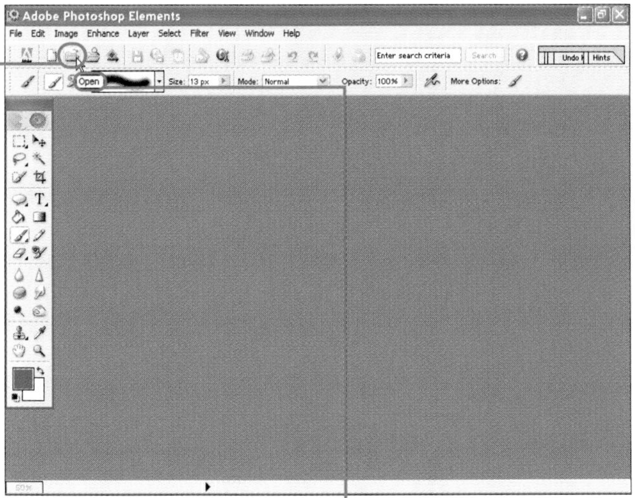

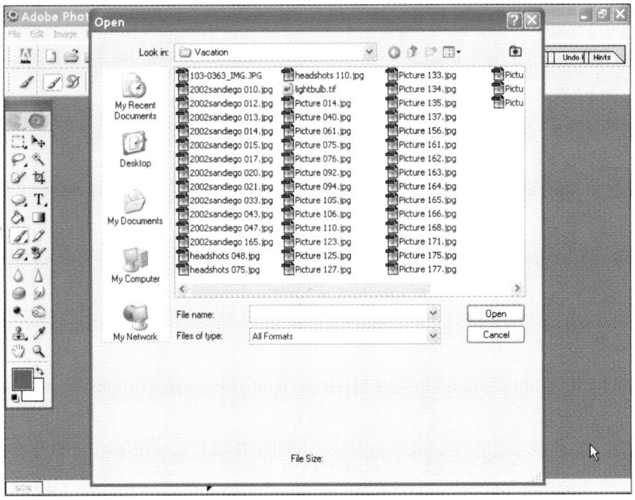

1 Place over a button in the Shortcuts bar and hold it there.

■ A small box appears that describes the shortcut.

2 Click the button.

■ Elements executes the command.

■ The following are a few of the commands accessible on the Shortcuts bar:

- Open
- Print
- Save
- Quick Fix
- Save for Web
- Attach to E-mail

UNDO COMMANDS

You can undo multiple commands by using the Undo History palette, which allows you to correct mistakes.

The Undo History palette lists recently executed commands with the most recent command at the bottom.

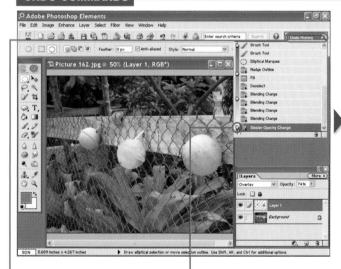

UNDO COMMANDS

1 Click the **Undo History** tab.

■ You can also click **Window** and then **Undo History**.

2 Click and drag the Undo History slider (▷) upward.

■ Alternatively, you can click a previous command in the Undo History palette.

■ Photoshop undoes the previous commands.

■ You can also click the Step Backward button (🔄) in the Shortcuts bar to undo commands.

REVERT AN IMAGE

You can revert an
image to the previously
saved state. This allows
you to start your image
editing over.

REVERT AN IMAGE

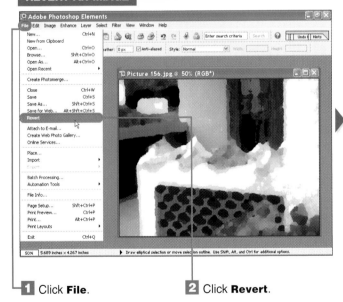

1 Click **File**.

2 Click **Revert**.

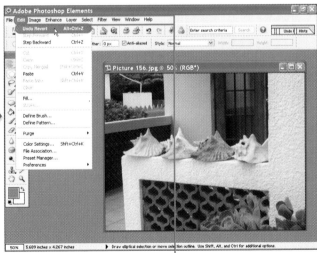

■ Photoshop reverts the
image to its previously saved
state.

■ You can click **Edit** and
then **Undo Revert** to return
to the unreverted state.

CHAPTER 3

Changing the Size of an Image

Would you like to change the size of your image? This chapter shows you how to change the on-screen size or print size, how to change the print resolution, and how to crop an image.

Hints

CHANGE THE ON-SCREEN SIZE OF AN IMAGE

You can change the size at which an image displays on your computer monitor so that viewers can see the entire image. Because you lose less clarity when you decrease an image's size than when you increase it, consider starting with an image that is too big rather than one that is too small.

Changing the on-screen size of an image involves resampling, which is the process of increasing or decreasing the number of pixels in an image.

CHANGE THE ON-SCREEN SIZE OF AN IMAGE

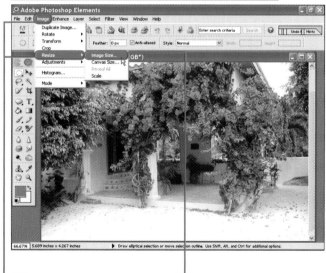

1 Click **Image**.

2 Click **Resize**.

3 Click **Image Size**.

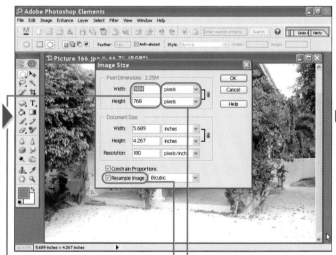

■ The Image Size dialog box appears listing the width and height of the image in pixels.

■ To resize by a certain percentage, click ∨ (⬍) and change the units to **percent**.

4 Click **Resample Image** (☐ changes to ☑).

What is the difference between an image's on-screen size and its print size?

On-screen size depends only on the number of pixels that make up an image. Print size depends on the number of pixels as well as the print resolution, which is the density of the pixels on a printed page. Higher resolutions print a smaller image, while lower resolutions print a larger image, given the same on-screen size.

96 ppi - Windows

72 ppi - Mac

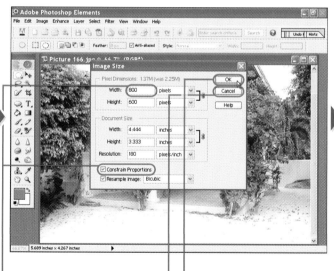

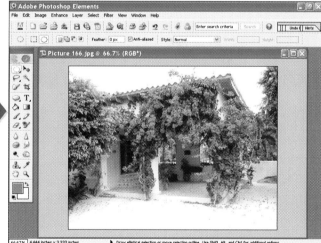

5 Type a size for a dimension.

■ You can click **Constrain Proportions** (☐ changes to ☑) to cause the other dimension to change proportionally.

6 Click **OK**.

■ You can restore the original dialog box settings without exiting the dialog box by holding down Alt (option) and clicking **Cancel**, which changes to **Reset**.

■ Elements resizes the image.

Note: Changing the number of pixels in an image can add blur. To sharpen a resized image, apply the Unsharp Mask filter, as covered in Chapter 11.

CHANGE THE PRINT SIZE OF AN IMAGE

You can change the printed size of an image to determine how it appears on paper.

CHANGE THE PRINT SIZE OF AN IMAGE

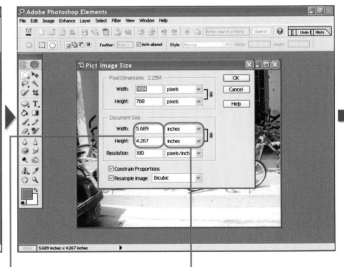

1 Click **Image**.

2 Click **Resize**.

3 Click **Image Size**.

■ The Image Size dialog box appears listing the current height and width of the printed image in the Document Size section.

■ You can click ✔ (⬍) to change the unit of measurement.

**How do I preview an
image's printed size?**

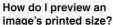

File
New... Ctrl+N
New from Clipboard
Open... Ctrl+O
Browse... Shft+Ctrl+O
Open As... Alt+Ctrl+O
Open Recent ▶
Create Photomerge...
Close Ctrl+W
Save
Save As... Shft+Ctrl+S
Save for Web... Alt+Shft+Ctrl+S
Revert
Attach to E-mail...
Create Web Photo Gallery...
Online Services...
Place...
Import ▶
Export
Batch Processing...
Automation Tools ▶
File Info...
Page Setup... Shft+Ctrl+P
Print Preview... Ctrl+P
Print... Alt+Ctrl+P
Print Layouts ▶
Exit Ctrl+Q

1 Click **File**.

2 Click **Print Preview**.

Print Preview

Tip: Sets image position and size on the current paper size, which you select in the Page Setup dialog box. To reposition the image, deselect Center Image and drag the image in the preview. Setting Scale greater than 100% may result in poor image quality.

OK
Cancel
Print...
Page Setup...
Help

Position
Top: 2.37 inches
Left: 1.867 inches
☑ Center Image

Scaled Print Size
Scale: 100% ☐ Scale to Fit Media
Height: 5.687 inches
Width: 4.267 inches
☑ Show Bounding Box
☐ Print Selected Area

☐ Show More Options

■ A dialog box displays how the image will print on the page.

■ You can type values in here to adjust the size and positioning of the image.

3 Click **OK** to apply the changes and exit the dialog box.

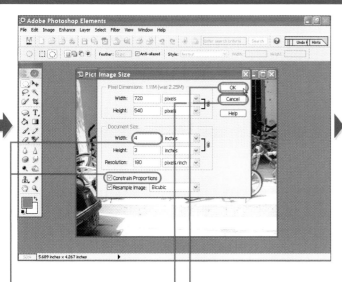

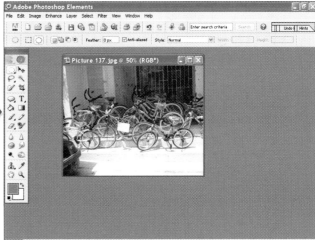

4 Type a size for a dimension.

■ You can click **Constrain Proportions** (☐ changes to ☑) to cause the other dimension to change proportionally.

5 Click **OK**.

■ You can restore the original dialog box settings by holding down **Alt** (**option**) and clicking **Cancel**, which changes to **Reset**.

■ Elements resizes the image.

Note: Changing the number of pixels in an image can add blur. To sharpen a resized image, apply the Unsharp Mask filter, as covered in Chapter 11.

49

CHANGE THE RESOLUTION OF AN IMAGE

You can change the print resolution of an image to increase or decrease the print quality.

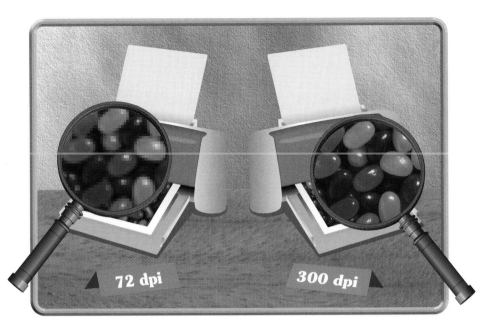

72 dpi   300 dpi

The resolution, combined with the number of pixels in an image, determines the size of a printed image.

The greater the resolution, the better the image looks on the printed page — up to a limit, which varies with the type of printer.

CHANGE THE RESOLUTION OF AN IMAGE

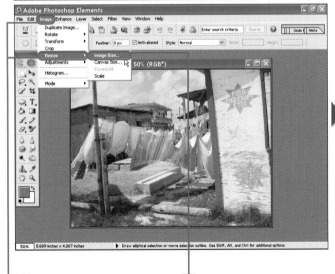

1 Click **Image**.

2 Click **Resize**.

3 Click **Image Size**.

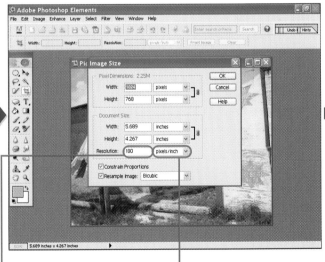

■ The Image Size dialog box appears listing the current resolution of the image.

■ You can click ⌄ (⬍) to change the resolution units.

What is the relationship between resolution, on-screen size, and print size?

To determine the printed size of a Photoshop image, you can divide the on-screen size by the resolution. If you have an image with an on-screen width of 480 pixels and a resolution of 120 pixels per inch, the printed width is 4 inches.

480 pixels/120 pixels per inch
=4 inches

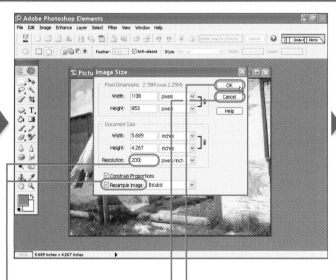

4 Type a new resolution.

■ You can click **Resample Image** (☐ changes to ☑) to adjust the number of pixels in your image and keep the printed dimensions fixed.

5 Click **OK**.

■ You can restore the original dialog box settings by holding down **Alt** (**option**) and clicking **Cancel**, which changes to **Reset**.

■ In this example, because the change in resolution changes the number of pixels in the image, the on-screen image changes in size while the print size stays the same.

CHANGE THE CANVAS SIZE OF AN IMAGE

You can alter the
canvas size of an
image in order to
change its
rectangular shape
or add blank space
around its borders.

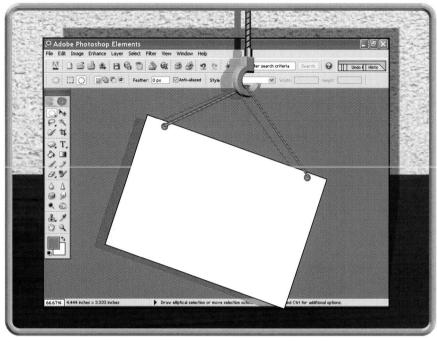

The *canvas* is the
area on which an
image sits. Changing
the canvas size is
one way to crop an
image, or add
matting (blank space)
around an image.

The Crop tool
gives you an
alternative to
changing the
canvas size.
See the section
"Crop an Image"
for more
information.

CHANGE THE CANVAS SIZE OF AN IMAGE

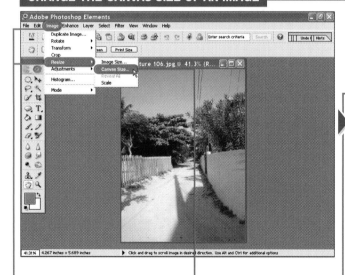

■1 Click **Image**.

■2 Click **Resize**.

■3 Click **Canvas Size**.

■ The Canvas Size dialog
box displays, listing the
current dimensions of
the canvas.

■ You can click ⌄ (⬍)
to change the unit of
measurement.

Why would I want to change the canvas size instead of using the Crop tool?

You may find changing the canvas size useful when you want to change the size of an image precisely. You can specify the exact number of pixels that Elements adds or subtracts around the border. With the Crop tool, you may find it more difficult to make changes with pixel precision.

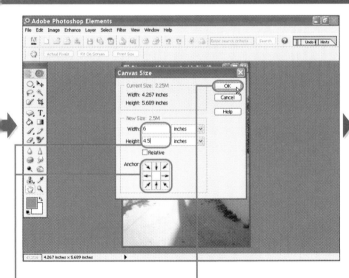

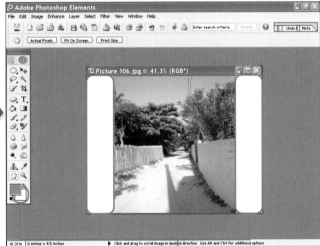

4 Type the new canvas dimensions.

■ You can modify in which directions Elements changes the canvas size by selecting an anchor point.

5 Click **OK**.

*Note: If you decrease a dimension, Elements displays a dialog box asking whether you want to proceed. Click **Proceed**.*

■ Elements changes the image's canvas size.

■ Because the middle anchor point was selected in this example, the canvas size changes equally on opposite sides.

■ Elements fills any new canvas space with the background color — in this case, white.

CROP AN IMAGE

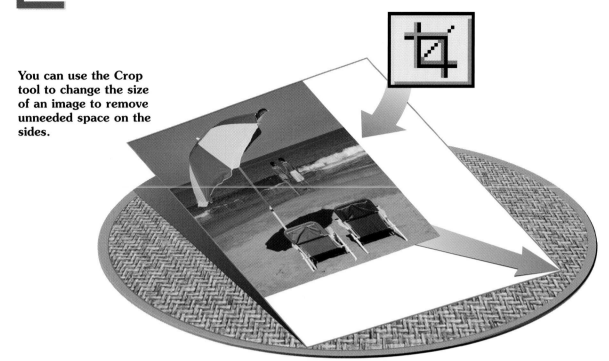

You can use the Crop tool to change the size of an image to remove unneeded space on the sides.

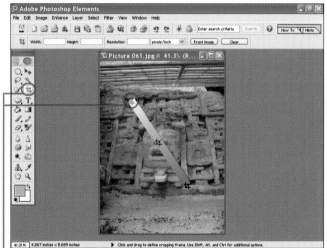

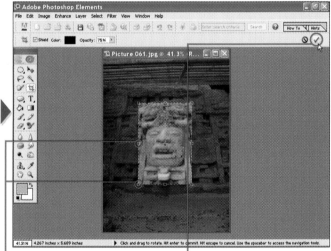

1 Click the Crop tool (▢).

2 Click and drag your cursor (▢) to select the area of the image you want to keep.

■ You can also crop an image by changing its canvas size.

Note: See the section "Change the Canvas Size of an Image" for more information.

3 Click and drag the side and corner handles (□) to adjust the size of the cropping boundary.

■ You can click and drag inside the cropping boundary to move it without adjusting its size.

4 Click ✓ or press Enter (Return).

■ To exit the cropping process, you can click the No button (⊘) or press Esc (⌘ + .).

**How do I increase the area of
an image using the Crop tool?**

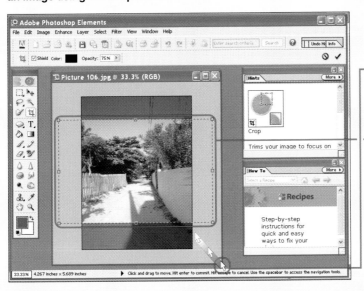

1 Click and drag the bottom
right corner of the image window
to enlarge the window and add
empty space around the image.

2 Using the steps in this
section, apply the Crop tool so
that the cropping boundary extends
beyond the borders of the image.

■ When you apply cropping,
the image canvas enlarges.

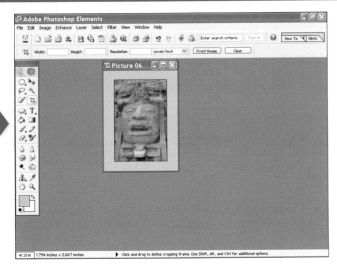

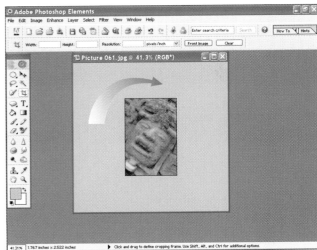

■ Elements crops the
image, deleting the pixels
outside the cropping
boundary.

ROTATE THE CROPPING AREA

1 Perform steps **1** to **3** on
the previous pages.

2 Click and drag outside of
the boundary lines.

3 Click ✓ or press `Enter`
(`Return`).

■ Elements crops the
boundary and rotates the
image.

CHAPTER 4

Making Selections

Do you want to move, color, or transform parts of your image independently from the rest of the image? The first step is to make a selection. This chapter shows you how.

SELECT WITH THE MARQUEE TOOLS

You can select a rectangular or elliptical area of your image by using the Marquee tools. Then you can move, delete, or stylize the selected area using other Photoshop commands.

SELECT WITH THE MARQUEE TOOLS

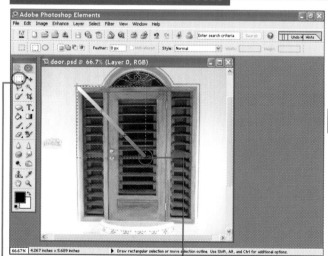

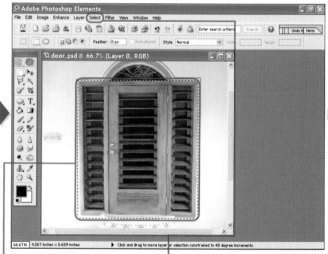

USING THE RECTANGULAR MARQUEE TOOL

1 Click the Rectangular Marquee tool (▦).

2 Click and drag diagonally inside the image window.

■ You can hold down **Shift** while you click and drag to create a square selection.

■ Elements selects a rectangular portion of your image.

■ You can now perform other commands on the selection.

■ You can move your selection by clicking inside it and dragging.

■ You can deselect a selection by clicking **Select** and then **Deselect**.

How do I customize the Marquee tools?

You can customize the Marquee tools (and)
by using the text fields and menus in the Options bar.

Feather

Typing in a Feather value
softens your selection
edge — which means that
Elements partially selects
pixels near the edge.

Style

The Style list lets you
define your Marquee tool
as a fixed size.

Width and Height

You define the fixed
dimensions in the Width
and Height boxes.

Feather: 10 px   Anti-aliased   Style: Fixed Size   Width: 200 px   Height: 300 px

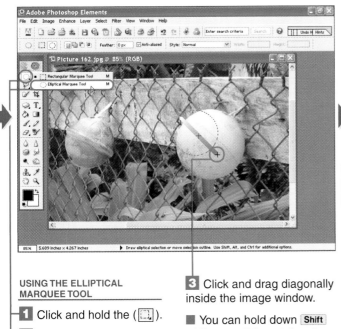

USING THE ELLIPTICAL MARQUEE TOOL

1 Click and hold the ( ).

2 From the menu that
appears, click the Elliptical
Marquee tool ( ).

3 Click and drag diagonally
inside the image window.

■ You can hold down Shift
while you click and drag to
create a circular selection.

■ Elements selects an
elliptical portion of your
image.

■ You can now perform
other commands on the
selection.

■ You can move your
selection by clicking inside
it and dragging.

■ You can deselect a
selection and start over by
clicking **Select** and then
Deselect.

SELECT WITH THE LASSO TOOLS

You can create oddly shaped selections with the Lasso tools. Then you can move, delete, or stylize the selected area using other Photoshop commands.

You can use the regular Lasso tool to create curved selections. The Polygonal Lasso tool lets you easily create a selection made up of many straight lines.

SELECT WITH THE LASSO TOOL

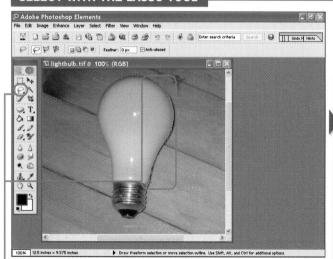

USING THE REGULAR LASSO

1 Click the Lasso tool (⊘).

2 Click and drag with your cursor (⌀) to make a selection.

■ To accurately trace a complicated edge, you can magnify that part of the image with the Zoom tool (🔍).

Note: See Chapter 2 for more on the Zoom tool.

3 Drag to the beginning point and release the mouse button.

■ If you release before you hit the beginning point, Elements encloses the selection for you with a straight line.

■ The selection is now complete.

What if my Lasso selection is not as precise as I want it to be?

You may find selecting complicated outlines with the Lasso tool () difficult, even with the steadiest of hands. To fix an imprecise Lasso selection, you can

■ Deselect the selection by clicking **Select** and then **Deselect** and try again.

■ Try to fix your selection. See the section "Add to or Subtract from a Selection" for more information.

■ Switch to the Magnetic Lasso. See the section "Select with the Magnetic Lasso Tool" for more on the use of this tool.

■ Use a graphics tablet instead of a mouse.

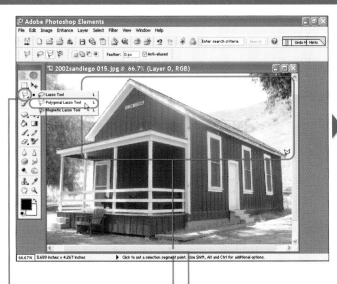

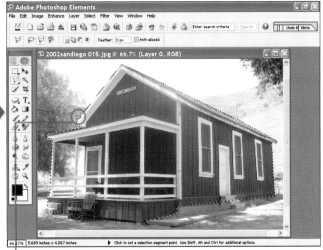

USING THE POLYGONAL LASSO

1 Click and hold 🔲.

2 Click the Polygonal Lasso tool (🔲) in the box that appears.

3 Click multiple times along the border of the area you would like to select.

4 To complete the selection, click the starting point.

■ You can also double-click anywhere in the image, and Elements adds a final straight line connected to the starting point.

■ The selection is now complete.

■ You can achieve a polygonal effect with the regular Lasso tool by pressing **Alt** (**option**) and clicking to make your selection.

SELECT WITH THE MAGNETIC LASSO TOOL

You can select elements of your image that have well-defined edges quickly and easily with the Magnetic Lasso tool.

The Magnetic Lasso works best when the element you are trying to select contrasts sharply with its background.

SELECT WITH THE MAGNETIC LASSO TOOL

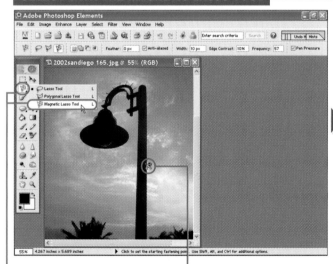

■1 Click and hold the ⬠.

■2 Click the Magnetic Lasso tool (🔲) from the box that appears.

■3 Click the edge of the object you want to select.

■ This creates a beginning anchor point.

■4 Drag your cursor (🔲) along the edge of the object.

■ The Magnetic Lasso's path snaps to the edge of the element as you drag.

■ To help guide the lasso, you can click to add anchor points as you go along the path.

How can I adjust the precision of the Magnetic Lasso tool?

You can use the Options bar to adjust the Magnetic Lasso tool's precision:

Width

The number of nearby pixels the lasso considers when creating a selection.

Edge Contrast

How much contrast is required for the lasso to consider something an edge.

Frequency

The frequency of the anchor points.

Width: 10 px   Edge Contrast: 10%   Frequency: 57

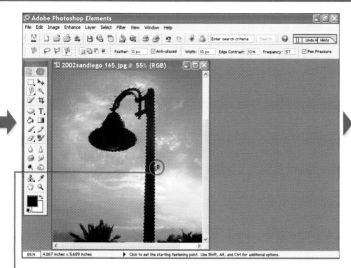

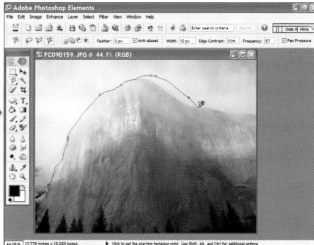

5 Click the beginning anchor point to finish your selection.

■ Alternatively, you can double-click anywhere in the image and Elements completes the selection for you.

■ The path is complete.

■ This example shows that the Magnetic Lasso is less useful for selecting areas where you find little contrast between the image and its background.

SELECT WITH THE MAGIC WAND TOOL

You can select groups of similarly colored pixels with the Magic Wand tool. You may find this useful if you want to remove an object from a background.

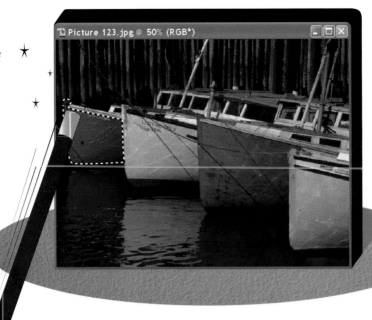

You can control how similar in color pixels must be for the wand to select them by typing a tolerance value.

SELECT WITH THE MAGIC WAND TOOL

1 Click the Magic Wand tool (✦).

2 Type a number from 0 to 255 into the Tolerance field.

■ To select a narrow range of colors, type a small number; to select a wide range of colors, type a large number.

3 Click the area you want to select inside the image.

■ Elements selects the pixel you clicked, plus any similarly colored pixels near it.

**With what type of images
does the Magic Wand tool
work best?**

The Magic Wand tool ()
works best with images that
have areas of solid color. The
Magic Wand tool is less helpful
with images that contain subtle
shifts in color or color
gradients.

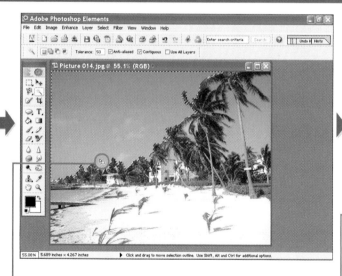

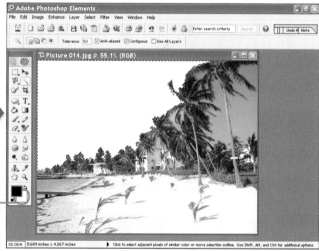

4 To add to your selection,
press **Shift** and click
elsewhere in the image.

■ Photoshop adds to your
selection.

5 To delete the selected
pixels, press **Delete**.

■ Elements replaces the
pixels with the background
color.

■ In this example, Elements
replaces the pixels with
white.

■ If you make the selection
in a layer, the deleted
selection becomes
transparent.

PAINT A SELECTION

You can select oddly shaped areas in your image by painting with the Selection Brush. By customizing the size and hardness of the brush, you can accurately trace edges that are curved or not well defined.

PAINT A SELECTION

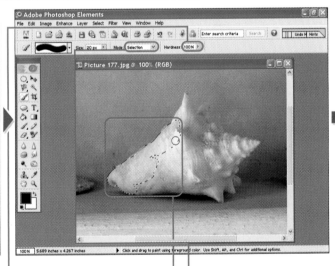

SELECT WITH THE SELECTION BRUSH

1 Click the Selection Brush tool (🖌).

2 Click ▶.

3 Click and drag △ to specify a size.

■ You can also type a size.

4 Type a hardness from 0 to 100 percent.

■ A smaller hardness produces a softer selection edge.

5 Click ▶ (♦) and click **Selection**.

6 Click and drag to paint a selection.

How do I paint a mask with the Selection Brush?

The Selection Brush's Mask option allows you to define the area that is *not* selected in your image, also known as *masking*. One advantage of a mask is it allows you to see the soft edges painted by a soft selection brush.

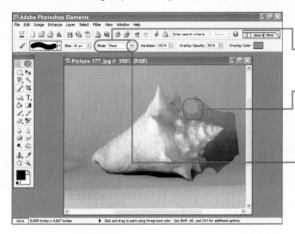

1 Click ⌄ (✦) in the Options bar, and then click **Mask**.

2 Click and drag to define the mask.

■ By default, the masked area shows up as a see-through red color.

■ To turn a painted mask into a selection, click ⌄ (✦) in the Options bar, and then click **Selection**.

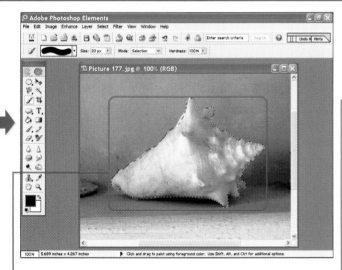

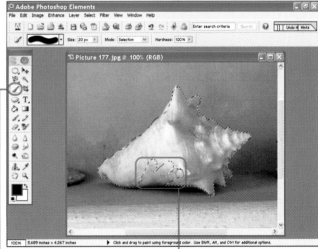

7 Click and drag multiple times to paint a selection over the entire object.

■ Elements creates a selection.

■ You can change the brush settings as you paint to select different types of edges in your object.

DESELECT WITH THE SELECTION BRUSH

1 Click 🖉.

2 Press and hold **Alt** (**option**).

3 Click and drag where you want to remove the selection area.

■ Elements removes the selection.

SELECT ALL THE PIXELS IN AN IMAGE

You can select all the pixels in an image by using a single command. This lets you perform a command on the entire image, such as copying it to a different image window.

SELECT ALL THE PIXELS IN AN IMAGE

1 Click **Select**.

2 Click **All**.

■ You can also press **Ctrl** + **A** (**⌘** + **A**) to select all the pixels in an image.

■ Elements selects the entire image window.

■ You can delete your image by pressing **Delete**.

■ To copy your image, press **Ctrl** + **C** (**⌘** + **C**).

■ To paste your image, press **Ctrl** + **V** (**⌘** + **V**).

MOVE A SELECTION BORDER

You can move a selection border if your original selection is not in the intended place.

MOVE A SELECTION BORDER

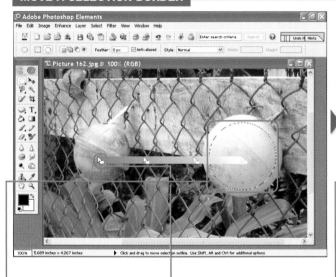

1 Make a selection with a selection tool (▢, ◌, or ⬩).

Note: To learn more about the various selection tools, see the previous sections in this chapter.

2 Click and drag inside the selection.

■ The selection border moves.

■ You can temporarily hide a selection by clicking **View** and then **Selection**.

ADD TO OR SUBTRACT FROM A SELECTION

You can add to or subtract from your selection by using various selection tools.

ADD TO A SELECTION

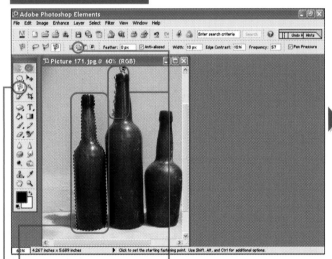

1 Make a selection using one of Elements' selection tools.

■ The selection in this example illustrates the use the Magnetic Lasso tool.

2 Click a selection tool.

Note: See the previous sections in this chapter to select the appropriate tool for your image.

3 Click the Add to Selection button (▣).

4 Select the area you want to add.

5 Complete the selection by closing the path.

■ The original selection enlarges.

■ You can enlarge the selection further by repeating steps **2** to **5**.

■ You can also add to a selection by pressing `Shift` as you make your selection.

What tools can I use to add to or subtract from a selection?

You can use any of the Marquee, Lasso, or Magic Wand tools, discussed in previous sections in this chapter, to add to or subtract from a selection. All three have Add to Selection and Subtract from Selection buttons available in the Options bar when you select them. You can also subtract using the Selection Brush by pressing **Alt** (**option**) as you click and drag.

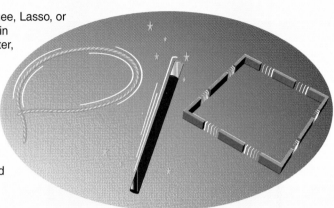

SUBTRACT FROM A SELECTION

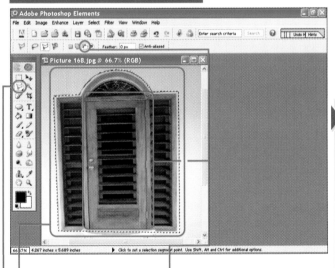

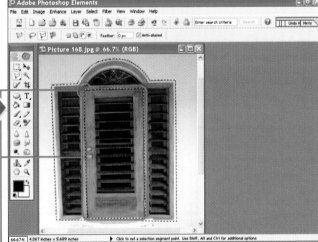

1 Make a selection using one of Elements' selection tools.

■ The selection in this example illustrates the use of the Polygonal Lasso tool.

2 Click a selection tool.

3 Click the Subtract from Selection button ( ).

4 Select the area you want to subtract.

5 Complete the selection by closing the path.

■ Elements deselects, or subtracts, the selected area.

■ You can subtract other parts of the selection by repeating steps **2** to **5**.

■ You can also subtract from a selection by holding down **Alt** (**option**) as you make your selection.

EXPAND OR CONTRACT A SELECTION

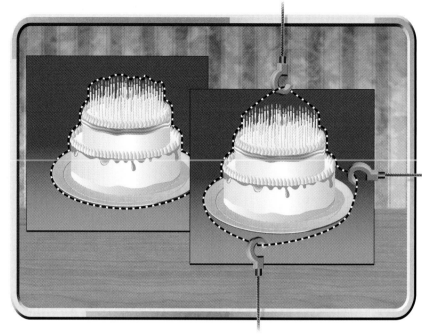

You can expand or contract a selection by a set number of pixels. This lets you easily fine-tune your selections.

You can expand or contract a selection up to 100 pixels at a time.

EXPAND A SELECTION

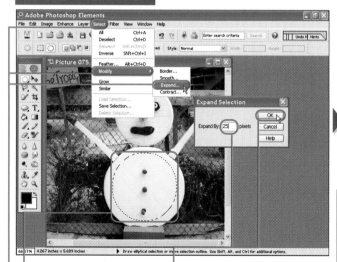

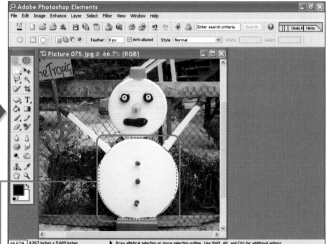

■1 Make a selection using one of Elements' selection tools.

■2 Click **Select**.

■3 Click **Modify**.

■4 Click **Expand**.

■ The Expand Selection dialog box appears.

■5 Type a value in the Expand By field.

■6 Click **OK**.

■ Elements expands the selection by the specified number of pixels.

■ You can repeat steps 2 to 6 to expand a selection further.

How can I smooth the edges of a selection?

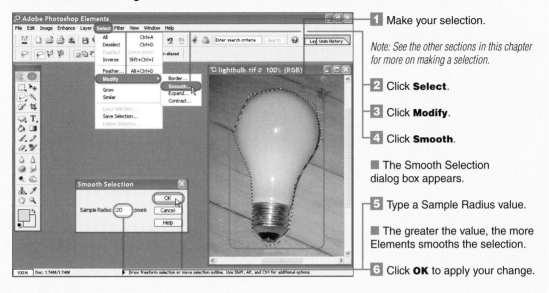

1 Make your selection.

Note: See the other sections in this chapter for more on making a selection.

2 Click **Select**.

3 Click **Modify**.

4 Click **Smooth**.

■ The Smooth Selection dialog box appears.

5 Type a Sample Radius value.

■ The greater the value, the more Elements smooths the selection.

6 Click **OK** to apply your change.

CONTRACT A SELECTION

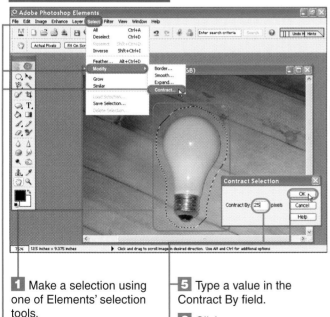

1 Make a selection using one of Elements' selection tools.

2 Click **Select**.

3 Click **Modify**.

4 Click **Contract**.

5 Type a value in the Contract By field.

6 Click **OK**.

■ Elements contracts the selection by the number of pixels specified.

■ You can repeat steps **2** to **6** to contract a selection further.

INVERT A SELECTION

You can invert a selection to deselect what is currently selected and select everything else. This is useful when you want to select a background around an object.

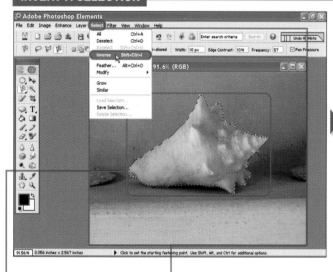

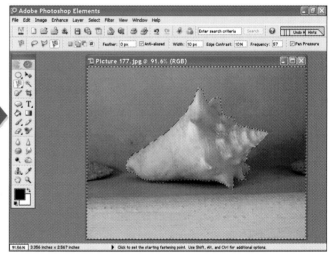

1 Make a selection using one of Elements' selection tools.

2 Click **Select**.

3 Click **Inverse**.

■ Elements inverts the selection.

■ You can press `Delete` to delete the inverted selection.

GROW A SELECTION

You can increase the size of your selection using the Grow command, which is useful when you want to include similarly colored, neighboring pixels in your selection.

The strength of the Grow command depends on the current tolerance setting of the Magic Wand tool. For more information, see "Select with the Magic Wand Tool."

GROW A SELECTION

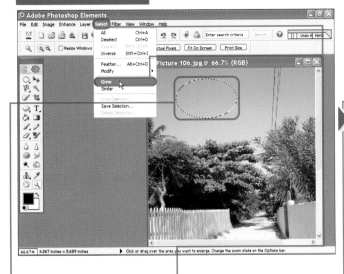

1 Make a selection using one of Elements' selection tools.

2 Click **Select**.

3 Click **Grow**.

■ The selection expands to include similarly colored pixels contiguous with the current selection.

■ To include noncontiguous pixels as well, you can click **Select** and then **Similar**.

CHAPTER 5

Manipulating Selections

Making a selection defines a specific area of your Photoshop image. This chapter shows you how to move, stretch, erase, and manipulate your selection in a variety of ways.

PREVIEW

Rotate

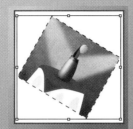

Skew & Distort

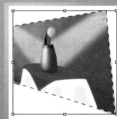

Copy & Paste

Scale

MOVE A SELECTION

You can move a selection by using the Move tool, which lets you rearrange elements of your image.

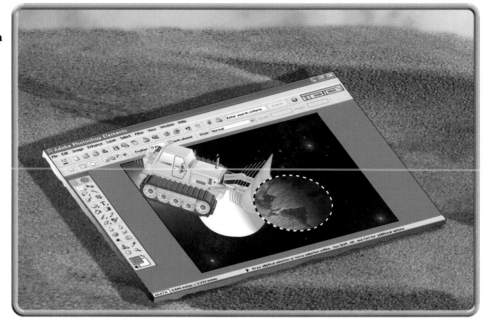

You can place elements of your image either in their own background or in layers. For details about layers, see Chapter 9.

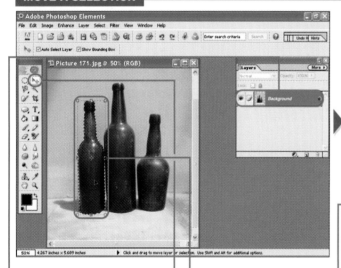

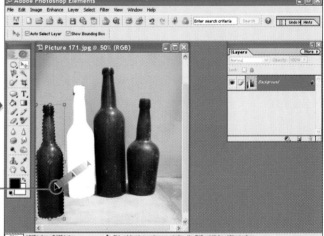

MOVE A SELECTION IN THE BACKGROUND

1 Click the Background layer in the Layers palette.

■ If you start with a newly scanned image, Elements makes the background layer the only layer.

2 Make a selection with a selection tool.

Note: See Chapter 4 for more on using selection tools and Chapter 9 for more on layers.

3 Click the Move tool ( ).

4 Click inside the selection and drag.

■ Elements fills the original location of the selection with the current background color.

■ In this example, white is the default background color.

How do I move a selection in a straight line?

Hold down the `Shift` key while you drag with the Move tool (). Doing so constrains the movement of your selection horizontally, vertically, or diagonally — depending on the direction you drag.

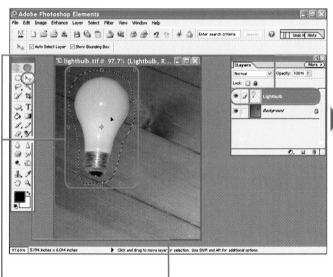

MOVE A SELECTION IN A LAYER

1 Click a layer in the Layers menu.

2 Make a selection with a selection tool.

Note: See Chapter 4 for more on using selection tools and Chapter 9 for more on layers.

3 Click ⊕.

4 Click inside the selection and drag.

■ Elements moves the selection.

■ Elements fills the original location of the selection with transparent pixels.

■ Unlike the background — Elements' opaque default layer — layers can include transparent pixels.

COPY AND PASTE A SELECTION

You can copy a selection and make a duplicate of it somewhere else in the image.

COPY AND PASTE A SELECTION

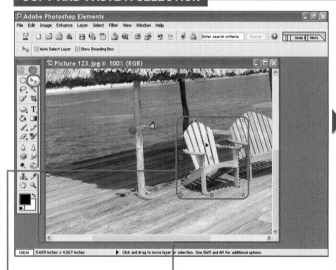

USING THE KEYBOARD AND MOUSE

1 Make a selection with a selection tool.

Note: See Chapter 4 for more on using selection tools.

2 Click ⊞.

3 Press **Alt** (**option**) while you click and drag the selection.

4 Release the mouse button to "drop" the selection.

■ Elements creates a duplicate of the selection, which appears in its new location.

How can I copy a selection from one window to another?

Click 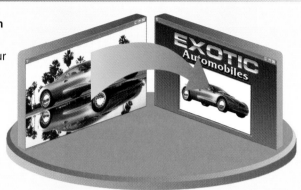 and click and drag your selection from one window to another. You can also copy selections between windows by using the Copy and Paste commands in the Edit menu.

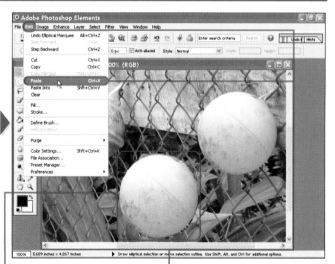

USING THE COPY AND PASTE COMMANDS

1 Make a selection with a selection tool.

Note: See Chapter 4 for more on using selection tools.

2 Click **Edit**.

3 Click **Copy**.

4 Using a selection tool, select where you want to paste the copied element.

■ If you do not select an area, Elements pastes the copy over the original.

5 Click **Edit**.

6 Click **Paste**.

■ Elements pastes the copy onto the selection area.

DELETE A SELECTION

You can delete a
selection to remove
elements from your
image.

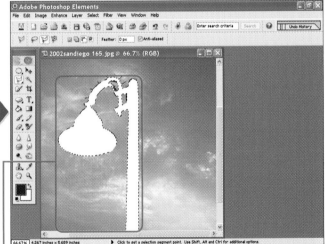

1 Make a selection with a
selection tool.

*Note: See Chapter 4 for more on
using selection tools.*

2 Press Delete .

■ Elements deletes the
selection.

■ If you are working in the
background layer, the empty
selection fills with the
background color — in this
example, white, the default
background color.

■ If you are working in
a nonbackground layer,
deleting a selection turns the
selected pixels transparent.

You can rotate a selection to tilt or turn an element upside down in your image.

ROTATE A SELECTION

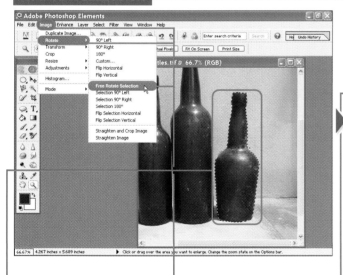

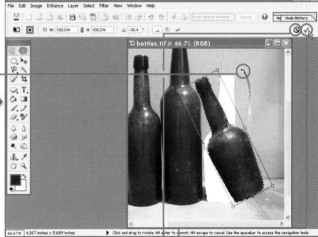

1 Make a selection with a selection tool.

Note: See Chapter 4 for more on using selection tools.

2 Click **Image**.

3 Click **Rotate**.

4 Click **Free Rotate Selection**.

5 Click and drag to the side of the selection.

■ The selection rotates.

6 Click ✓ or press `Enter` (`Return`) to commit the rotation.

■ You can click ⊘ or press `Esc` (⌘ + .) to cancel.

SCALE A SELECTION

You can scale a selection to make it larger or smaller. Scaling allows you to adjust or emphasize parts of your image.

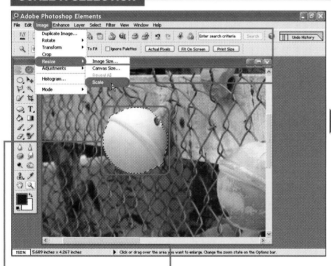

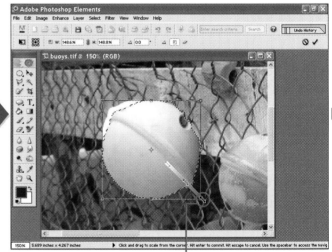

1 Make a selection with a selection tool.

Note: See Chapter 4 for more on using selection tools.

2 Click **Image**.

3 Click **Resize**.

4 Click **Scale**.

■ A rectangular box with handles on the sides and corners surrounds the selection.

5 Click and drag a corner handle to scale both the horizontal and vertical axes.

How do I scale both dimensions proportionally?

Hold down `Shift` while you click and drag a corner handle of your selection. The two axes of your selection grow or shrink proportionally.

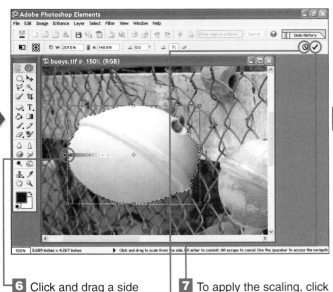

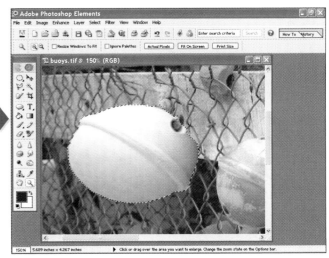

6 Click and drag a side handle to scale one axis at a time.

7 To apply the scaling, click 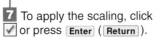 or press `Enter` (`Return`).

■ To cancel, you can click ⊘ or press `Esc` (⌘+ .).

■ Elements scales the selection to the new dimensions.

SKEW OR DISTORT A SELECTION

You can transform a selection using the Skew or Distort command. This lets you stretch elements in your image into interesting shapes.

SKEW A SELECTION

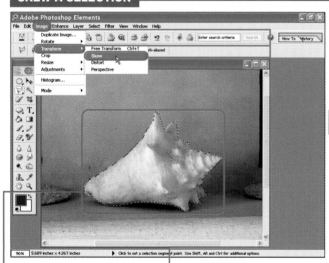

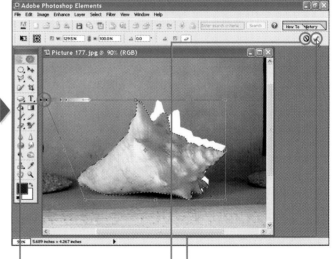

1 Make a selection with a selection tool.

Note: See Chapter 4 for more on using selection tools.

2 Click **Image**.

3 Click **Transform**.

4 Click **Skew**.

■ A rectangular box with handles on the sides and corners surrounds the selection.

5 Click and drag a handle to skew the selection.

■ Because the Skew command works along a single axis, you can drag either horizontally or vertically.

6 To apply the skewing, click ✓ or press **Enter** (**Return**).

■ To cancel, you can click ⊘ or press **Esc** (⌘ + .).

How can I undo my skewing or distortion?

You can click **Edit** and then **Undo** to undo the last handle adjustment you made. This is an alternative to clicking , which cancels the entire Skew or Distort command.

DISTORT A SELECTION

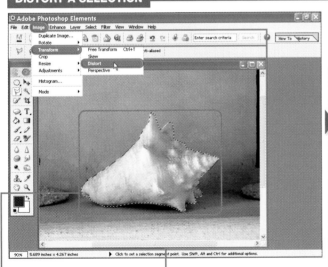

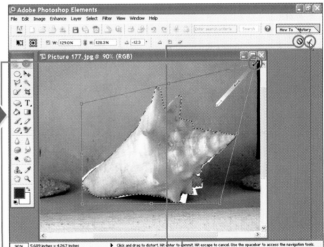

1 Make a selection with a selection tool.

Note: See Chapter 4 for more on using selection tools.

2 Click **Image**.

3 Click **Transform**.

4 Click **Distort.**

■ A rectangular box with handles on the sides and corners surrounds the selection.

5 Click and drag a handle to distort the selection.

■ The Distort command works independently of the selection's different axes; you can drag a handle both vertically and horizontally.

6 To apply the distortion, click ✓ or press **Enter** (**Return**).

■ To cancel, you can click ⊘ or press **Esc** (⌘ + .).

USING THE FREE TRANSFORM TOOL

You can use the Free Transform tool to scale and rotate a selection all at once.

To apply the scale or rotate commands independently, see the section "Scale a Selection" or "Rotate a Selection."

USING THE FREE TRANSFORM TOOL

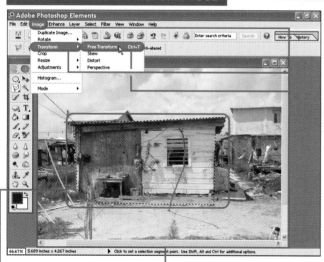

1 Make a selection with a selection tool.

Note: See Chapter 4 for more on using selection tools.

2 Click **Image**.

3 Click **Transform**.

4 Click **Free Transform**.

■ A rectangular box with handles on the sides and corners surrounds the selection.

5 Click and drag a corner handle to scale the selection in two dimensions.

■ You can also click and drag a side handle to scale it in one dimension.

**How can I easily switch between
the different transformation tools?**

You can click the transformation
buttons located in the Options bar.
This lets you switch between the
Rotate (⊿), Scale (⬛), and Skew
(⬕) tools. You can also type
numeric scaling dimensions and
rotation amounts in the Options
bar to transform your selection
precisely.

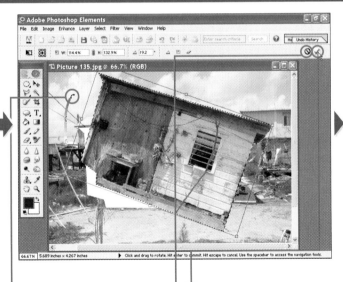

6 Click and drag outside
the selection to rotate it.

7 To apply the distortion,
click ✔ or press **Enter**
(**Return**).

■ To cancel, you can click
⊘ or press **Esc** (⌘ + .).

■ Elements applies your
changes.

FEATHER THE BORDER OF A SELECTION

You can feather a selection's border to create soft edges.

To create a soft edge around an object, you must first select the object, feather the selection border, and then delete the part of the image that surrounds your selection.

FEATHER THE BORDER OF A SELECTION

SELECT AND FEATHER THE IMAGE

1 Make a selection with a selection tool.

Note: See Chapter 4 for more on using selection tools.

2 Click **Select**.

3 Click **Feather**.

■ The Feather Selection dialog box appears.

4 Type a pixel value to determine the softness of the edge.

5 Click **OK**.

TEACH YOURSELF

What happens if I feather a selection and then apply a filter or other command to it?

Elements applies the command only partially to pixels near the edge of the selection.

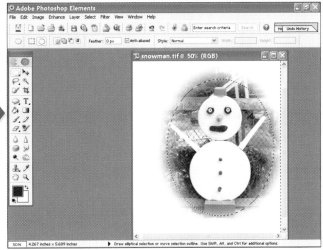

DELETE THE SURROUNDING BACKGROUND

6 Click **Select**.

7 Click **Inverse**.

■ The selection inverts, but remains feathered.

8 Press Delete.

■ You can now see the effect of the feathering.

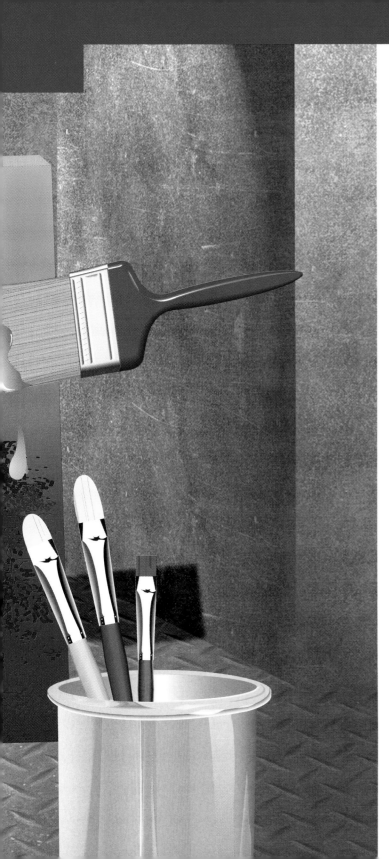

CHAPTER 6

Painting and Drawing with Color

Want to add splashes, streaks, or solid areas of color to your image? Elements offers a variety of tools with which you can add almost any color imaginable. This chapter introduces you to those tools and shows you how to choose your colors.

SELECT THE FOREGROUND AND BACKGROUND COLORS

You can select two colors to work with at a time in Elements — a foreground color and a background color. Painting tools such as the Paintbrush apply foreground color. You apply the background color when you use the Eraser tool, enlarge the image canvas, or cut pieces out of your image.

SELECT THE FOREGROUND COLOR

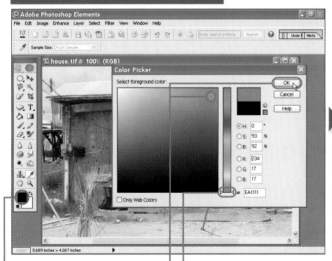

1 Click the Foreground Color box (■).

■ The Color Picker dialog box appears.

■ To change the range of colors that appears in the color box, click and drag the slider (◁).

2 To select a foreground color, click the color you want in the color box.

3 Click **OK**.

■ The selected color appears in the Foreground Color box.

4 Click a painting tool in the toolbox.

■ This example uses the Paintbrush tool (✐).

Note: To learn more about painting tools, see the section "Using the Paintbrush Tool."

5 Click and drag your cursor (○) to apply the color.

How do I reset the foreground and background colors?

Click the Default icon (■) to the lower left of the Foreground and Background icons. Doing so resets the colors to black and white. You can also click the Switch icon (↰) to swap the foreground and background colors.

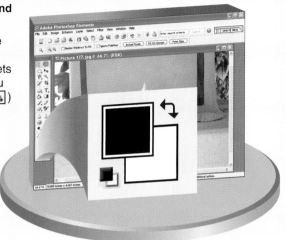

SELECT THE BACKGROUND COLOR

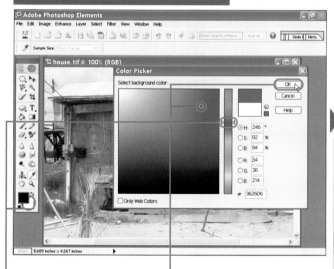

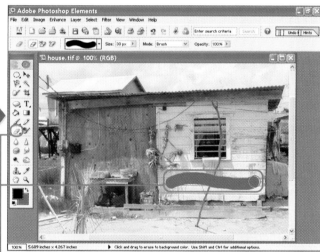

1 Click the Background Color box (☐).

■ To change the range of colors that appears in the color box, click and drag ◁.

2 To select a background color, click the color you want in the color box.

3 Click **OK**.

4 Click the Eraser tool (⌿).

5 Click and drag your cursor (○).

■ The tool erases by painting with the background color.

Note: In non-background layers, the eraser turns pixels transparent. See Chapter 9 for a full discussion of layers.

SELECT A WEB-SAFE COLOR

You can select one of the 216 Web-safe colors as a foreground or background color. A Web-safe color displays accurately in all graphical Web browsers, no matter what type of monitor or operating system a user has.

See Chapter 14 for information about saving images with Web-safe colors.

SELECT A WEB-SAFE COLOR

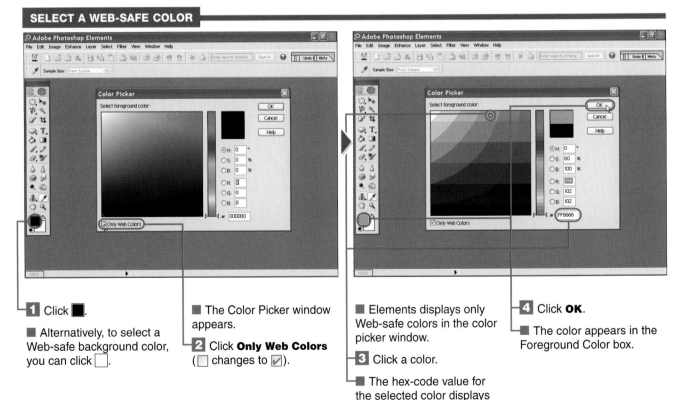

1 Click ■.

■ Alternatively, to select a Web-safe background color, you can click □.

■ The Color Picker window appears.

2 Click **Only Web Colors** (□ changes to ☑).

■ Elements displays only Web-safe colors in the color picker window.

3 Click a color.

■ The hex-code value for the selected color displays here.

4 Click **OK**.

■ The color appears in the Foreground Color box.

SELECT A COLOR WITH THE EYEDROPPER TOOL

You can select a color from an open image with the Eyedropper tool. The Eyedropper tool enables you to paint using a color already present in your image.

SELECT A COLOR WITH THE EYEDROPPER TOOL

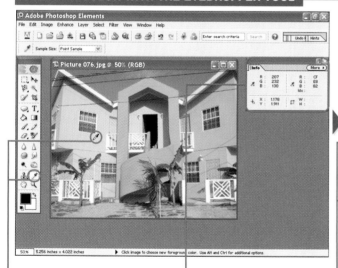

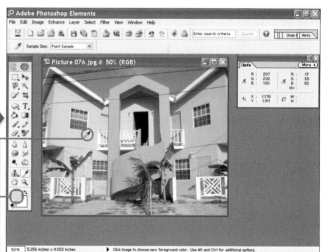

■1 Click the Eyedropper tool (✐).

■2 Place ✐ over an open image.

■ You can see color values in the Info palette as you move ✐.

■ You can click **Window** and then **Info** to open the Info palette.

■3 Click to select the color of the pixel beneath the tip of the ✐.

■ The color becomes the new foreground color.

■ To select a new background color, you can press **Alt** (**option**) as you click in step **3**.

SELECT A COLOR WITH THE SWATCHES PALETTE

You can select a color with the Swatches palette. The Swatches palette lets you choose from a set of commonly used colors.

SELECT A COLOR WITH THE SWATCHES PALETTE

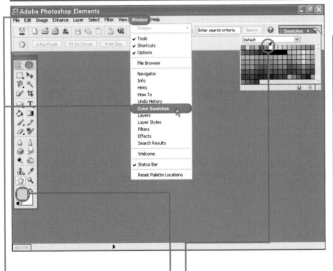

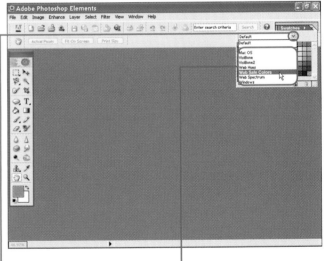

SELECT A COLOR

1 Click **Window**.

2 Click **Color Swatches**.

■ The Swatches palette opens.

3 Click a color swatch to select a foreground color.

■ The color becomes the new foreground color.

■ To select a background color, press `Ctrl` (⌘) as you click in step **3**.

CHANGE THE SWATCH SELECTION

1 Click ✔ (▼).

2 Click a swatch set.

■ The set of swatches appears in the Swatches palette.

You can add custom
colors to the Swatches
palette. This enables you
to store commonly used
colors for a project and
easily select these colors
later.

STORE A COLOR IN THE SWATCHES PALETTE

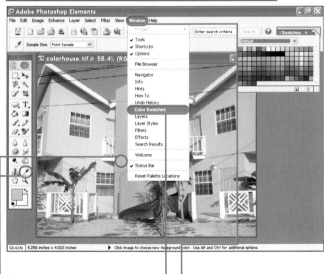

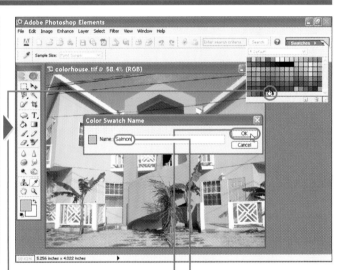

1 Click ![eyedropper].

2 Click inside the image to select a color.

3 Click **Window**.

4 Click **Color Swatches**.

■ The Swatches palette opens.

5 Place ![eyedropper] over an empty area of the Swatches palette (![eyedropper] changes to ![bucket]).

6 Click to add the color.

■ The Color Swatch Name dialog box appears.

7 Type a name for the new color swatch.

8 Click **OK**.

■ Elements adds the color as a new swatch.

USING THE PAINTBRUSH TOOL

You can use the Paintbrush tool to add color to your image. You may find the paintbrush useful for applying bands of color.

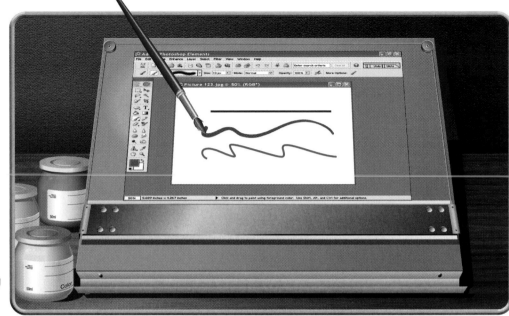

To limit where the paintbrush applies color, create a selection before using painting. For details, see Chapter 4.

USING THE PAINTBRUSH TOOL

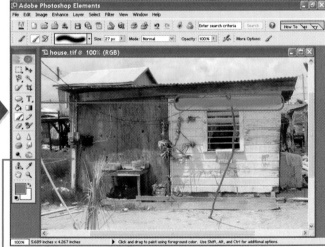

APPLY THE PAINTBRUSH

1 Click the Paintbrush tool (☑).

2 Click ■ to select a color with which to paint.

Note: For details, see the section "Select the Foreground and Background Colors."

3 Click the Brush ⊡ and select a brush size and type.

4 Click and drag ○ to apply the foreground color to the image.

■ To undo the most recent brush stroke, you can click **Edit** and then **Undo Paintbrush**.

Note: To undo more than one brush stroke, see Chapter 2 to learn how to use the Undo History palette.

How do I paint thin lines?

Use the Pencil tool (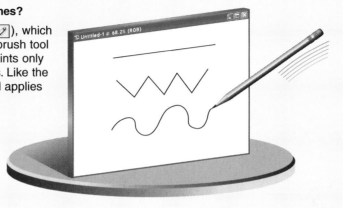), which is similar to the Paintbrush tool (⬛) except that it paints only thin, hard-edged lines. Like the Paintbrush, the Pencil applies the foreground color.

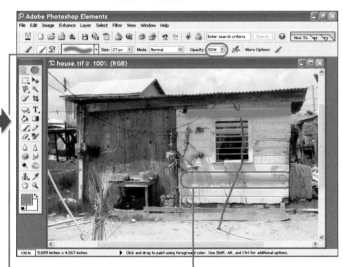

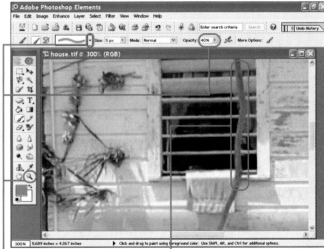

5 Type a percentage value to change the opacity of the brush strokes.

■ Alternatively, you can click the Opacity ▶ and adjust the slider.

6 Click and drag ◯ to apply the semitransparent paintbrush.

PAINT A DETAIL

1 Click the Brush ⋮ to select a small brush size.

■ You can specify an opacity to apply a semitransparent color.

2 Use the Zoom tool to focus on a detail in your image.

Note: See Chapter 2 for more about the Zoom tool.

3 Click and drag to apply color to the detail.

■ Elements applies the color.

CHANGE BRUSH STYLES

You can select from a
variety of predefined
brush styles to apply
color in different ways.
You can also create a
custom brush style.

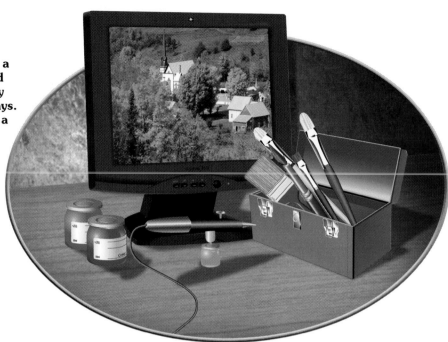

**SELECT FROM A
PREDEFINED SET**

1 Click ✐.

2 Click the Brush ⬚.

3 Click ⬇ (⬚).

4 Click a set of brushes.

■ The set appears in the
brush menu.

5 Click a brush style to
select it.

■ The cursor changes to the
new brush shape.

*Note: To apply the brush, see the
section "Using the Paintbrush Tool."*

**How can I make
a brush apply dots
instead of a line?**

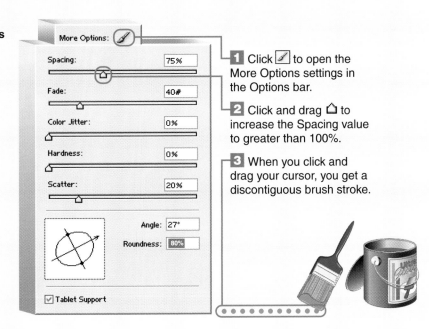

1 Click ✎ to open the
More Options settings in
the Options bar.

2 Click and drag △ to
increase the Spacing value
to greater than 100%.

3 When you click and
drag your cursor, you get a
discontiguous brush stroke.

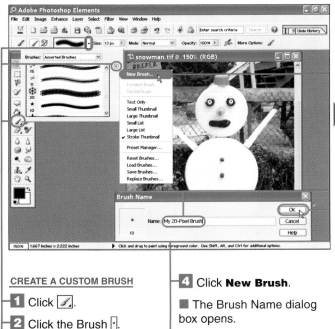

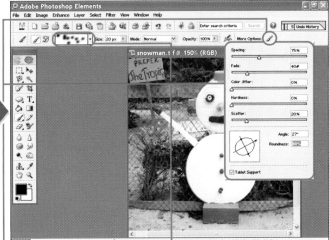

CREATE A CUSTOM BRUSH

1 Click ✎.

2 Click the Brush ⊡.

3 Click ⊙.

4 Click **New Brush**.

■ The Brush Name dialog
box opens.

5 Type a brush name.

6 Click **OK**.

7 Click the More Options
(✎) button.

8 Click and drag the sliders
(△) and type values to
define the new brush
attributes in the dialog
box that appears.

9 Press **Enter (Return)** to
close the options box.

■ The brush style appears
in the brush menu.

*Note: To apply the brush, see the
section "Using the Paintbrush Tool."*

103

USING THE PAINT BUCKET TOOL

You can fill areas in your image with solid color using the Paint Bucket tool.

You can set the Paint Bucket's Tolerance value to determine what range of colors the paint bucket affects in the image when you apply it.

USING THE PAINT BUCKET TOOL

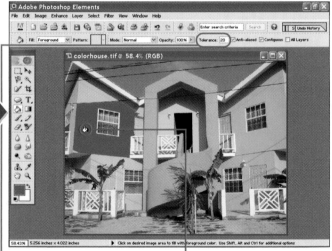

SELECT THE PAINT BUCKET TOOL

1 Click the Paint Bucket tool (⬚).

2 Click ⬚ to select a color for painting.

Note: For details, see the section "Select the Foreground and Background Colors."

SET THE TOLERANCE

3 Type a Tolerance value from 0 to 255.

4 Click inside the image.

■ Elements fills an area of the image with the foreground color.

104

How can I reset a tool to the default settings?

Click the tool's icon on the far left side of the Options bar and select **Reset Tool** from the menu that appears. This resets the opacity to 100%, the blending mode to Normal, and other attributes to their startup values. You can also click **Reset All Tools** from the menu to reset all the Elements tools to their default settings.

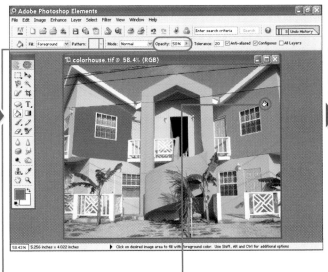

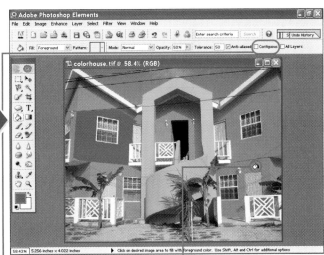

SET IMAGE OPACITY

5 To fill an area with a semitransparent color, type a percentage value of less than 100 in the Opacity field.

6 Click inside the image.

■ Elements fills an area with see-through paint.

FILL NONCONTIGUOUS AREAS

7 To fill similar areas throughout the image, uncheck the **Contiguous** option (☑ changes to ☐).

8 Click inside the selection.

■ Elements fills similar areas of the image, even if they are not contiguous with the clicked pixel.

USING THE IMPRESSIONIST BRUSH

You can apply artistic styles to your image with the Impressionist Brush. The brush creates its effect by blending existing colors in an image together.

The Impressionist Brush does not add any foreground or background color to your image.

USING THE IMPRESSIONIST BRUSH

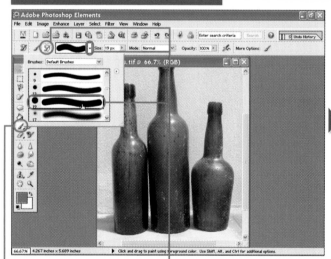

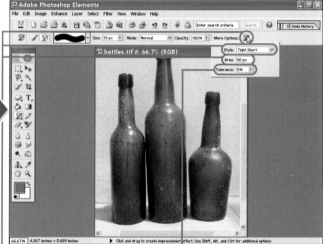

APPLY THE BRUSH

1 Click the Brush tool ( ).

2 In the Options bar, click the Impressionist Brush tool ( ).

3 Click the Brush .

4 Click a brush size and type.

5 Click the More Options ( ) button.

6 Click here to select a style to control the brush shape.

7 Type a size to adjust the area affected beneath the brush stroke.

8 Click here to select a tolerance to control what pixels the brush affects.

■ A low tolerance affects only pixels similar in color to the one initially clicked; a high tolerance affects more pixels.

How do I decrease the effects that I apply with the Impressionist Brush?

An easy way is to decrease the opacity of the brush. Doing this causes Elements to maintain more of the original image's features.

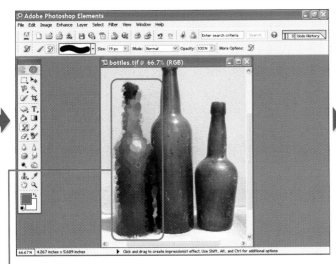

9 Click and drag the cursor (○) to apply the brush.

■ The colors blend to mimic the style of an impressionist painting.

CONSTRAIN THE BRUSH

10 Create a selection with a selection tool.

Note: See Chapter 4 for more information about selections.

11 Click and drag the cursor (○) inside the selection.

■ The brush effects are limited to the pixels inside the selection.

USING THE PATTERN STAMP

You can paint with a pattern using the Pattern Stamp tool. The tool gives you a free-form way to add repeating elements to your images.

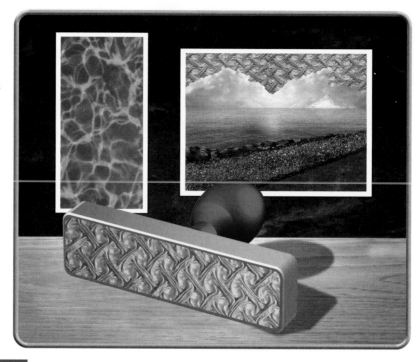

USING THE PATTERN STAMP

SELECT A PATTERN

1 Click the Clone Stamp ( ).

2 In the Options bar, click the Pattern Stamp ( ).

Note: The Pattern Stamp has a small checkerboard pattern next to it.

3 Click the Brush .

4 Select a brush size and type.

5 Click the Pattern .

6 Click a pattern to apply.

■ You can click **Aligned** (changes to) to make your different strokes paint the pattern as contiguous tiles.

108

How do I define a custom pattern?

You can define a rectangular selection in your image and have it added to the Pattern menu.

3 Click **Define Pattern**.

■ The Pattern Name dialog box appears.

4 Type a name for the pattern.

5 Click **OK**.

1 Select your custom pattern using the Rectangular Marquee.

Note: See Chapter 4 for more about selections.

2 Click **Edit**.

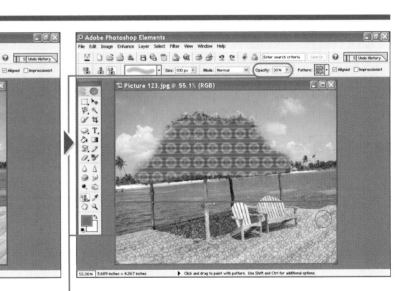

7 Click and drag ○ to apply the pattern.

■ The pattern appears where you click and drag.

APPLY A DIFFERENT OPACITY

8 Type a value of less than 100 in the Opacity box.

9 Click and drag ○ inside the selection to apply the pattern.

■ Decreasing the opacity applies a semitransparent pattern.

FILL A SELECTION

You can fill a selection with a solid or semitransparent color using the Fill command. Filling is an easy way to change the color of an object in your image.

See the section "Using the Paint Bucket Tool" if you want to fill adjacent pixels rather than a selected area.

FILL A SELECTION

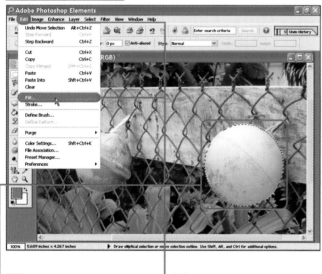

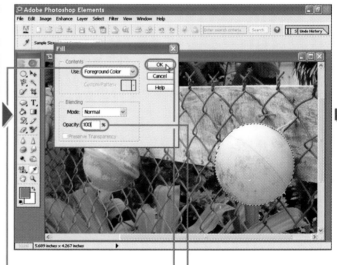

1 Define the area you want to fill using a selection tool.

Note: See Chapter 4 for more on using selection tools.

2 Click **Edit**.

3 Click **Fill**.

■ The Fill dialog box appears.

4 Click the ∨ (⬦) and select what you want to fill with.

■ You can decrease the opacity to fill with a semitransparent color or pattern.

5 Click **OK**.

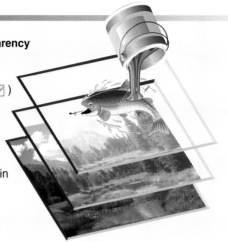

What does the Preserve Transparency option in the Fill dialog box do?

If you select **Preserve Transparency** (☐ changes to ☑) and perform a fill, Elements only fills pixels in the layer that *are not* transparent. Elements leaves transparent pixels alone. This option lets you easily color objects that exist by themselves in a layer.

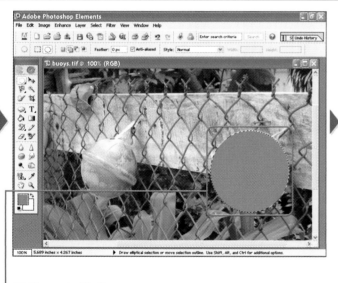

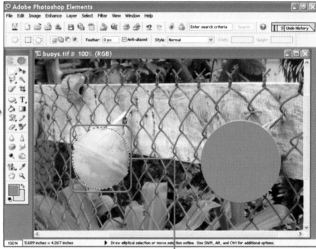

■ Elements fills the area.

■ You can select other areas and fill them with different colors.

■ This example uses a fill with the background color set to 30% opacity.

STROKE A SELECTION

You can use the Stroke command to draw a line along the edge of a selection. This can help you highlight objects in your image.

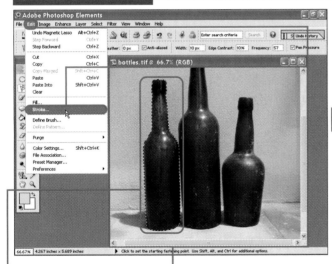

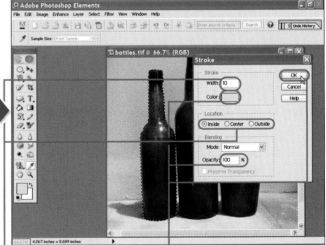

1 Select an area of the image with a selection tool.

Note: See Chapter 4 for more on using selection tools.

2 Click **Edit**.

3 Click **Stroke**.

■ The Stroke dialog box appears.

4 Type a width in pixels to determine the stroke thickness.

5 Click **Inside** to stroke a line on the inside of the selection, **Center** to stroke a line straddling the selection, or **Outside** to stroke a line on the outside of the selection (○ changes to ◉).

■ You can click the color box to define the color of the stroke.

■ You can change the opacity to apply a semitransparent stroke.

6 Click **OK**.

112

How do I add a colored border to the outside of my image?

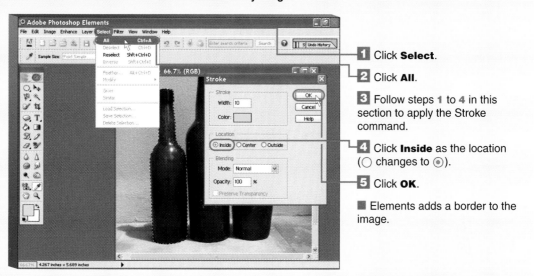

1 Click **Select**.

2 Click **All**.

3 Follow steps **1** to **4** in this section to apply the Stroke command.

4 Click **Inside** as the location (○ changes to ⊙).

5 Click **OK**.

■ Elements adds a border to the image.

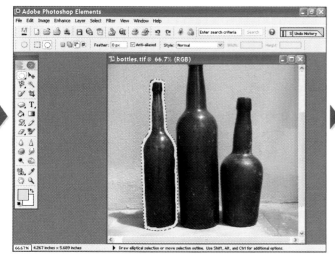

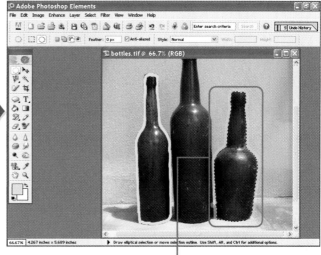

■ Elements strokes a line along the selection.

■ You can select other areas and stroke them using different settings.

■ This stroke was applied to the outside of the selection at 40% opacity.

DRAW A SHAPE

You can create solid shapes in your image using Elements' many shape tools. Shapes offer an easy way to add whimsical objects, labels, or buttons to an image.

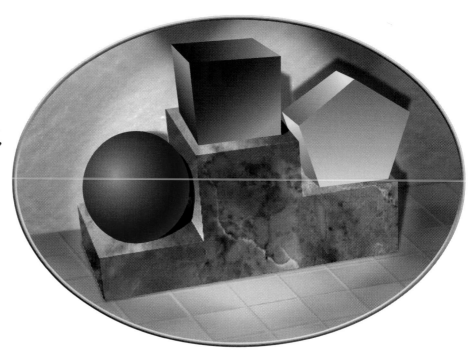

When you add a shape to an image, Elements places the shape in its own layer. This makes it easy to move and transform the shape later on. For more information about layers, see Chapter 9.

DRAW A SHAPE

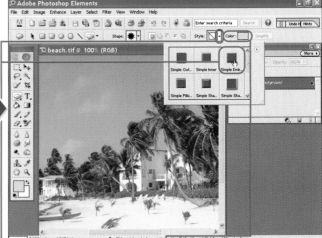

1 Click the Custom Shape tool (◻).

Note: The tool icon may differ, depending on what type of shape you drew last.

■ You can select from standard shapes in the Options bar.

2 Click the Shape ⊡.

3 Click a shape.

4 Press `Enter` (`Return`) to close the menu.

5 Click the Style ⊡.

6 Click a style for your shape.

■ Elements offers a variety of 3-D styles.

7 Press `Enter` (`Return`) to close the menu.

■ You can click the Color box (▢) to select a different shape color.

**How do I
resize a shape
after I draw it?**

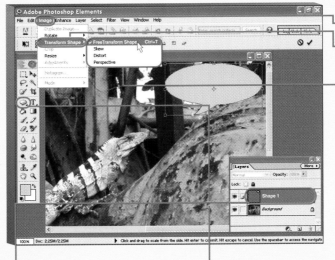

3 Click **Image**.

4 Click **Transform
Shape**.

5 Click a transform
command.

■ You can then resize
the shape just like you
would a selection.

*Note: See Chapter 5 for more
details on transformations.*

1 Click the
shape's layer.

2 Click the Custom
Shape tool (▱).

8 Click and drag your
cursor (+) to draw the
shape.

■ Elements places the
shape in its own layer.

*Note: For more about layers, see
Chapter 9.*

9 Click an overlay option.

■ In this example, Subtract
from shape area is selected.

10 Click and drag + to draw
another shape.

■ Elements applies your
overlay options.

115

DRAW A LINE

You can draw a straight line using Elements' Custom Shape tool. You can customize the line with arrows, giving you an easy way to point out elements in your image.

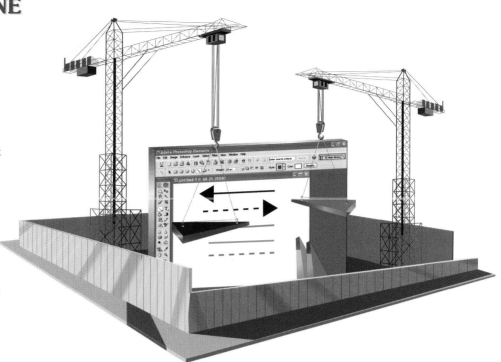

When you add a line to an image, Elements places the line in its own layer. This makes it easy to move and transform the line later on. For more information about layers, see Chapter 9.

DRAW A LINE

1 Click ⬜.

Note: The tool icon may differ, depending on what type of shape you drew last.

2 Click the Line tool (◥).

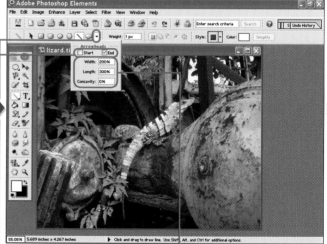

3 Click the tool ⬝.

4 Click **Start** or **End** to include arrowheads on your line (⬜ changes to ☑).

■ You can also specify the shape of the arrowheads by typing values here.

5 Press `Enter` (`Return`) to close the menu.

How do I access more custom shapes?

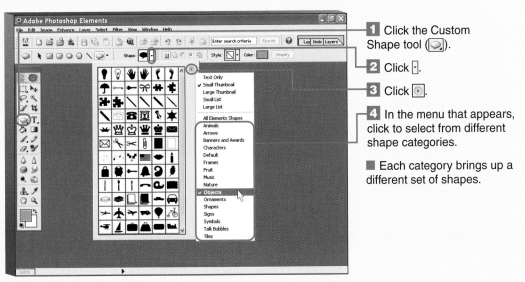

1 Click the Custom Shape tool (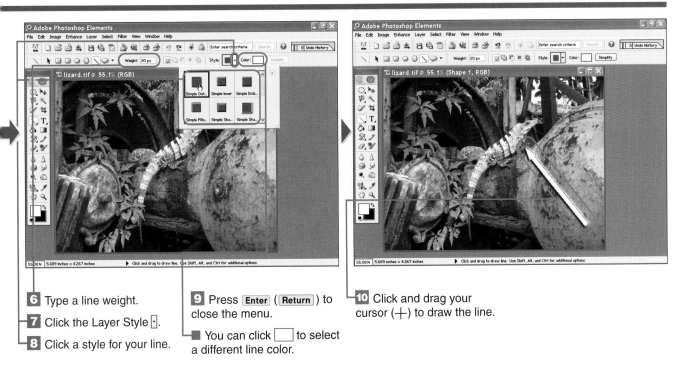).

2 Click [·].

3 Click [▸].

4 In the menu that appears, click to select from different shape categories.

■ Each category brings up a different set of shapes.

6 Type a line weight.

7 Click the Layer Style [·].

8 Click a style for your line.

9 Press **Enter** (**Return**) to close the menu.

■ You can click ☐ to select a different line color.

10 Click and drag your cursor (+) to draw the line.

APPLY A GRADIENT

You can apply a gradient, which is a blend from one color to another. This gives objects in your image a radiant or 3-D look.

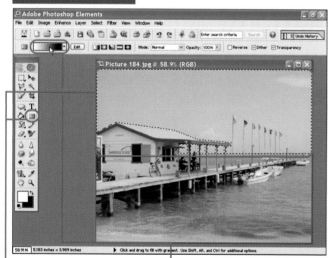

1 Make a selection.

Note: See Chapter 4 for more on making selections.

2 Click the Gradient tool (▣).

■ A linear gradient is the default. You can select different geometries in the Options bar.

3 Click the gradient swatch.

■ The Gradient Editor opens.

4 Click a preset gradient type from the top box.

■ You can define a custom gradient by using these settings.

5 Click **OK**.

118

TEACH YOURSELF

How can I highlight an object in my image using a gradient?

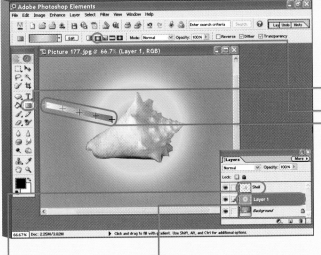

Note: For more information about layers, see Chapter 9.

3 Click .

4 Click the Radial Gradient button (▣).

5 Click and drag your cursor (╋) to create the gradient.

■ This highlights the object with a burst of color.

1 Place the object in its own layer.

2 Create a new layer below the object where you can create the gradient.

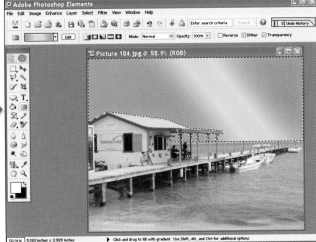

6 Click and drag your cursor (╋) inside the selection.

■ This defines the direction and transition of the gradient.

■ Dragging a long line with the tool produces a gradual transition.

■ Dragging a short line with the tool produces an abrupt transition.

■ Elements generates a gradient inside the selection.

CHAPTER 7

Adjusting Colors

Do you want to fine-tune the colors in your image — darken them, lighten them, or remove them completely? This chapter introduces the tools that let you do the trick.

color

The Brightness/ Contrast command provides a simple way to make adjustments to the highlights and shadows of your image.

To change the brightness or contrast of small parts of your image, use the Dodge or Burn tool. See "Using the Dodge and Burn Tools" in this chapter for details.

If you make a selection before performing the Brightness/Contrast command, changes only affect the selected pixels. Similarly, if you have a multilayered image, your adjustments only affect the selected layer. See Chapter 4 to make a selection and Chapter 9 for more on layers.

CHANGE BRIGHTNESS AND CONTRAST

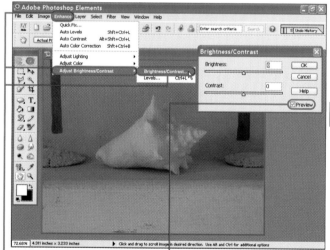

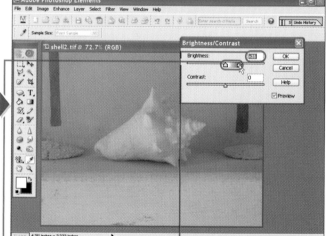

1 Click **Enhance**.

2 Click **Adjust Brightness/Contrast**.

3 Click **Brightness/Contrast**.

■ A dialog box opens with sliders set to 0.

4 To have your adjustments display in the image window as you make them, click **Preview** (☐ changes to ☑).

5 Click and drag the Brightness slider (△).

■ Drag △ to the right to lighten the image, or to the left to darken the image.

■ You can also lighten the image by typing a number from 1 to 100, or darken the image by typing a negative number from −1 to −100.

How can I adjust the contrast of an image automatically?

Click **Enhance**, and then **Auto Contrast**. Elements converts the very lightest pixels in the image to white and the very darkest pixels in the image to black. Making the highlights brighter and the shadows darker boosts the contrast, which can bring out details and improve the appearance of poorly exposed photographs.

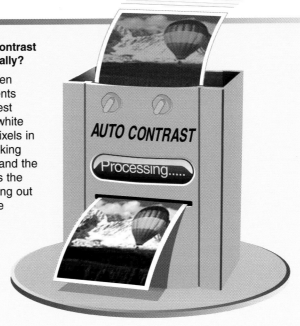

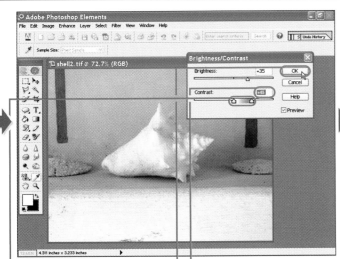

6 Click and drag the Contrast slider (△).

■ Drag △ to the right to increase the contrast, or to the left to decrease the contrast.

Note: Increasing contrast can bring out details in your image.

■ You can also increase the contrast by typing a number from 1 to 100, or decrease the contrast by typing a negative number from −1 to −100.

7 Click **OK**.

■ Elements applies the new brightness and contrast values.

USING THE DODGE AND BURN TOOLS

You can use the Dodge tool to brighten and the Burn tool to darken specific areas of an image.

Dodge is a photographic term that describes the diffusing of light when developing a film negative. *Burn* is a photographic term that describes the focusing of light when developing a film negative.

These tools are an alternative to the Brightness/Contrast command, which affects the entire image. To brighten or darken the entire image, see the section "Change Brightness and Contrast."

USING THE DODGE TOOL

1 Click the Dodge tool (⬛).

2 Click the Brush ⬝.

3 Click the brush that you want to use.

■ You can also select the range of colors you want to affect and the tool's exposure, or strength.

4 Click and drag your cursor (○) over the area that you want to lighten.

■ Elements lightens the area.

**How can I add extra
shadow to the bottom
of an object?**

Applying the Burn tool
with the Range set to
Shadows offers a useful
way to add shadows to
the shaded side of an
object. Likewise, you can
use the Dodge tool with
Range set to Highlights
to add highlights to the
lighted side of an object.

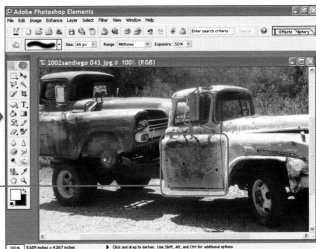

USING THE BURN TOOL

1 Click the Burn tool ( ).

■ You can select the brush,
the range of colors you want
to affect, and the tool's
exposure, or strength.

2 Click and drag ○ over
the area that you want to
darken.

■ Elements darkens the
area.

USING THE BLUR AND SHARPEN TOOLS

You can sharpen or blur specific areas of your image with the Sharpen and Blur tools. This allows you to emphasize or de-emphasize objects in a photo.

You can blur or sharpen the entire image by using one of the Blur or Sharpen commands located in Elements' Filter menu. See Chapter 11 for more information.

USING THE BLUR TOOL

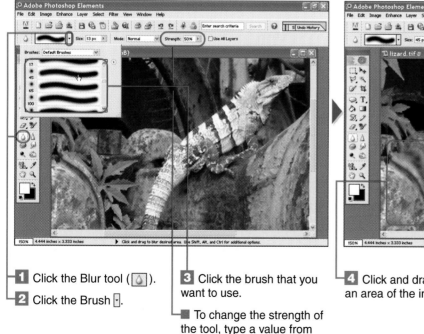

1 Click the Blur tool ().

2 Click the Brush ⬝.

3 Click the brush that you want to use.

■ To change the strength of the tool, type a value from 1% to 100%.

4 Click and drag ○ to blur an area of the image.

■ Elements blurs the area.

What is the Smudge tool?

The Smudge tool ()
is another tool in the
Elements toolbox. It
simulates dragging a
finger through wet paint,
shifting colors and blurring
your image.

USING THE SHARPEN TOOL

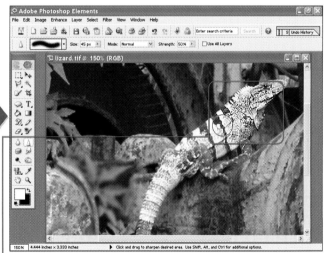

1 Click the Sharpen
tool (△).

2 Click the Brush ⬚ and
click the brush that you want
to use.

■ To change the strength of
the tool, type a value from
1% to 100%.

3 Click and drag ○ to
sharpen an area of the
image.

■ Elements sharpens the
area.

ADJUST LEVELS

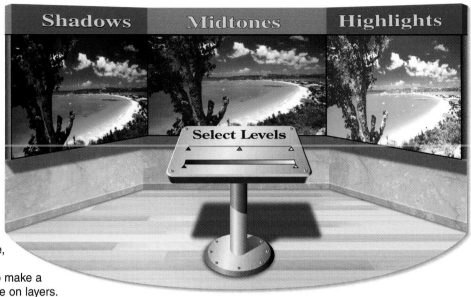

Shadows · Midtones · Highlights

Select Levels

The Levels command lets you make fine adjustments to the highlights, midtones, or shadows of an image.

Although more difficult to use, the Levels command offers more control over brightness than the Brightness/Contrast command covered in the section "Change Brightness and Contrast."

To affect only selected pixels, select them before performing the Levels command. Similarly, if you have a multilayered image, your adjustments only affect the selected layer. See Chapter 4 to make a selection and Chapter 9 for more on layers.

ADJUST LEVELS

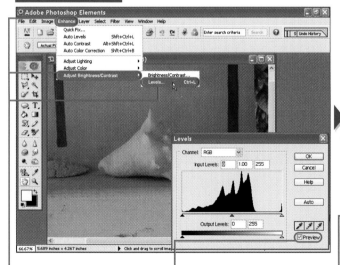

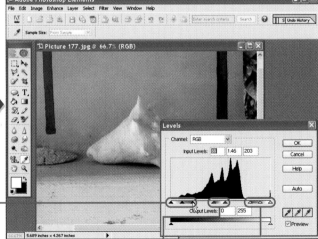

1 Click **Enhance**.

2 Click **Adjust Brightness/Contrast**.

3 Click **Levels**.

■ The Levels dialog box appears.

4 To display your adjustments in the image window as you make them, click **Preview** (☐ changes to ☑).

■ Use the Input sliders (△) to adjust an image's brightness, midtones, and highlights.

5 Click and drag ▲ to the right to darken shadows and increase contrast.

6 Click and drag △ to the left to lighten the bright areas of the image and increase contrast.

7 Click and drag ▲ to adjust the midtones of the image.

128

How do you adjust the brightness levels of an image automatically?

Click **Enhance** and then **Auto Levels**. Elements converts the very lightest pixels in the image to white and the very darkest pixels in the image to black. This command is similar to the Auto Contrast command and can quickly improve the contrast of an overly gray photographic image. See the section "Change Brightness and Contrast" for more information.

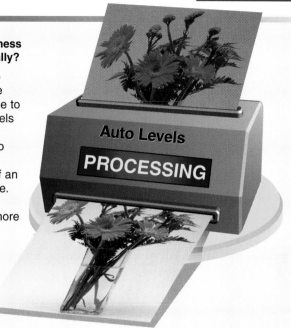

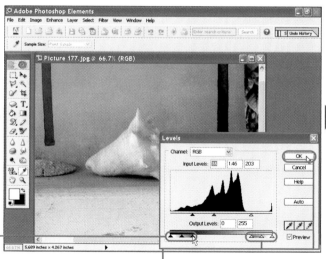

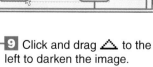

■ The Output sliders △ let you decrease the contrast while either lightening or darkening the image.

8 Click and drag ▲ to the right to lighten the image.

9 Click and drag △ to the left to darken the image.

10 Click **OK**.

■ Elements makes brightness and contrast adjustments to the image.

ADJUST HUE AND SATURATION

You can change the hue to shift the component colors of an image. You can change the saturation to adjust the color intensity in an image.

If you make a selection before performing the Hue/Saturation command, you only affect the selected pixels. Similarly, if you have a multilayered image, your adjustments only affect the selected layer. See Chapter 4 to make a selection and Chapter 9 for more on layers.

ADJUST HUE AND SATURATION

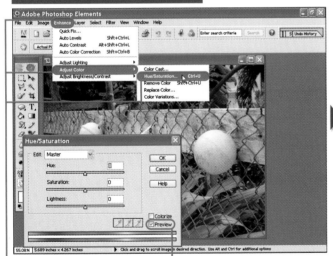

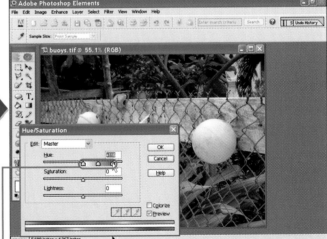

1 Click **Enhance**.

2 Click **Adjust Color**.

3 Click **Hue/Saturation**.

■ The Hue/Saturation dialog box appears.

4 To display your adjustments in the image window as you make them, click **Preview** (☐ changes to ☑).

5 Click and drag the Hue slider (⌂) to shift the colors in the image.

■ Dragging ⌂ left or right shifts the colors in different, and sometimes bizarre, ways.

■ In this example, adjusting the hue has changed the red to green.

How does the adjustment of an image's hues work?

When you adjust an image's hues in Elements, its colors shift according to their position on the standard color wheel. The color wheel is a graphical way of presenting colors in the visible spectrum.

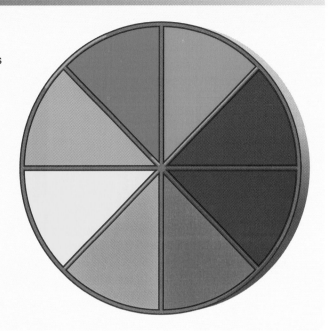

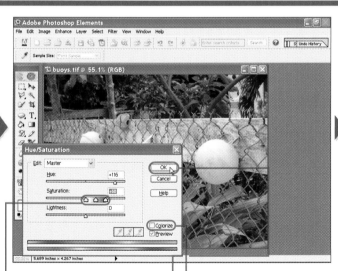

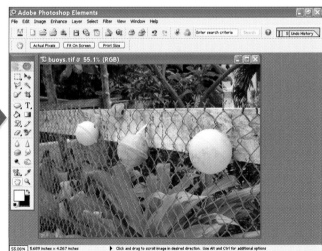

6 Click and drag the Saturation slider (⌂).

■ Dragging ⌂ to the right or to the left increases or decreases the intensity of the image's colors, respectively.

■ Clicking **Colorize** (☐ changes to ☑), turns the image — even a grayscale one — into a monotone, or one-color, image. You can adjust the color with the sliders.

7 Click **OK**.

■ Elements makes the color adjustments to the image.

The Variations command gives you a user-friendly interface with which to perform color adjustments in your image. The command allows you to change the color balance or the brightness.

If you make a selection before performing the Variations command, you only affect the selected pixels. Similarly, if you have a multilayered image, your adjustments only affect the selected layer. See Chapter 4 to make a selection and Chapter 9 for more on layers.

USING THE VARIATIONS COMMAND

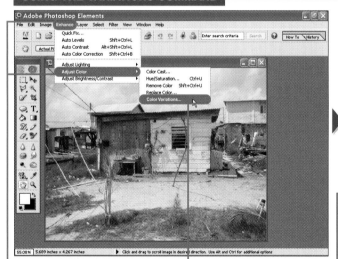

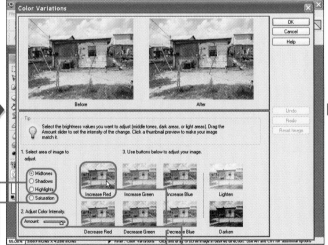

1 Click **Enhance**.

2 Click **Adjust Color**.

3 Click **Color Variations**.

■ The Color Variations dialog box appears.

4 Select a tonal range to apply effects to the different tones of your image (○ changes to ◉).

■ Alternatively, you can click **Saturation**, or strength of color (○ changes to ◉).

5 Click and drag the Amount △ left to make small adjustments, or right to make large adjustments.

6 To change the color in your image, click one of the **Increase** or **Decrease** thumbnails.

How can I undo color adjustments while using the Variations dialog box?

Increase thumbnail

Click an **Increase** thumbnail to undo a corresponding decrease command.

Decrease thumbnail

Click a **Decrease** thumbnail to undo a corresponding increase command.

Undo button

Click the **Undo** button to cancel the last color adjustment.

Reset Image button

Click the **Reset Image** button to revert the image to its original state — before you opened the dialog box.

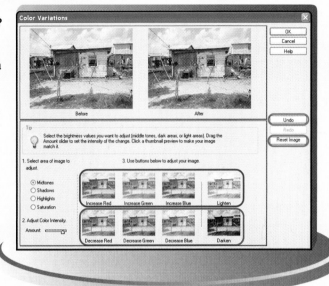

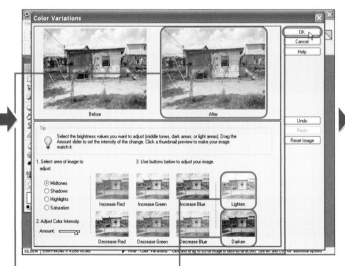

■ The result of the adjustment shows up in the After thumbnail.

■ To increase the effect, you can click the **Increase** or **Decrease** thumbnail again.

■ You can increase the brightness of the image by clicking **Lighten**.

■ You can decrease the brightness by clicking **Darken**.

7 Click **OK**.

■ Elements makes the color adjustments to the image.

USING THE SPONGE TOOL

You can use the Sponge tool to adjust the color saturation, or color intensity, of a specific area of an image.

To adjust the saturation of the entire image at once, see "Adjust Hue and Saturation."

USING THE SPONGE TOOL

DECREASE SATURATION

1 Click the Sponge tool ().

2 Click the Brush ⊡.

3 Click the brush that you want to use.

4 Click ⌄ (▤) and select **Desaturate**.

5 Click and drag the mouse (○) to decrease the saturation of an area of the image.

How can I easily convert a color image to grayscale?

Click **Enhance**, **Adjust Color**, and then **Remove Color**. This command effectively sets the saturation value of the image to 0, converting it to grayscale.

INCREASE SATURATION

1 Perform steps **1** to **3** on the previous page.

2 Click ⌄ (⬍) and select **Saturate**.

3 Click and drag ◯ to increase the saturation of an area of the image.

■ You can adjust the strength of the Sponge tool by typing a Flow setting from 1% to 100%.

REPLACE A COLOR

The Replace Color command lets you select one or more colors in your image and then change them using hue, saturation, and lightness controls.

If you make a selection before performing the Replace Color command, you only affect the selected pixels. Similarly, if you have a multilayered image, your adjustments only affect the selected layer. See Chapter 4 to make a selection and Chapter 9 for more on layers.

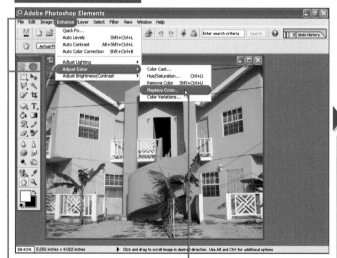

1 Click **Enhance**.

2 Click **Adjust Color**.

3 Click **Replace Color**.

■ The Replace Color dialog box appears.

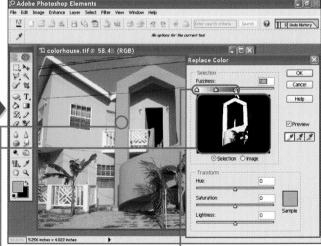

4 Click in the image to select a color.

■ The selected color and similar colors appear as white in the Selection preview.

5 Click and drag △ to specify the Fuzziness.

■ Dragging to the right selects more color.

■ Dragging to the left selects less color.

How can I replace more than one color?

You can press **Shift** and then click inside your image to add other colors to your selection. The white area inside the Selection box increases as you click. To deselect colors from your selection, press **Alt** (**option**) and then click a color inside your image.

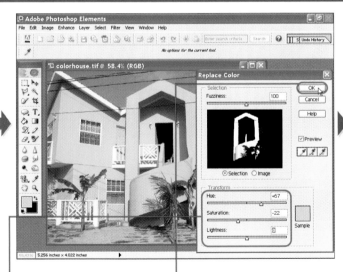

6 Click and drag the transform sliders (🖆) to change the colors inside the selected area.

Note: For details about these controls, see the section "Adjust Hue and Saturation."

7 Click **OK**.

■ Elements replaces the selected color.

EQUALIZE COLORS

You can use the Equalize command to redistribute the brightness values in your image. This can lighten an overly dark or gray photo.

Elements equalizes an image by finding the lightest and darkest colors in the image and converting them to white and black. It also redistributes the colors in between.

If you make a selection before performing the command, Elements asks whether you want to equalize only the selection or equalize the entire image based on the selection.

EQUALIZE COLORS

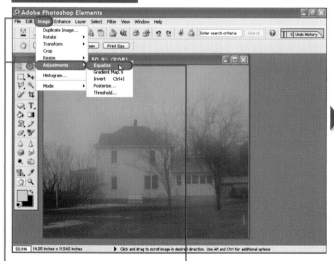

1 Click **Image**.

2 Click **Adjustments**.

3 Click **Equalize**.

■ Elements equalizes the colors in the image.

POSTERIZE COLORS

You can reduce the
number of colors in
your image using the
Posterize command,
which can give a
photographic image a
solid-color poster look.

If you make a selection
before performing the
Posterize command, you
only affect the selected
pixels. Similarly, if you have
a multilayered image, your
adjustments only affect the
selected layer. See Chapter
4 to make a selection and
Chapter 9 for more on
layers.

The Caribbean. For a Change.

Caribbean Airways

POSTERIZE COLORS

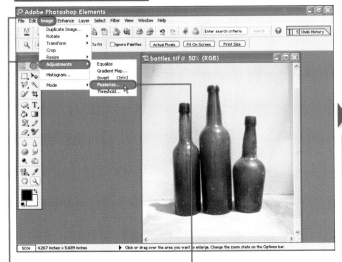

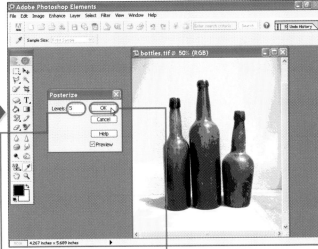

1 Click **Image**.

2 Click **Adjustments**.

3 Click **Posterize**.

■ The Posterize dialog box
appears.

4 Type the number of
levels.

■ More levels mean more
solid colors in the resulting
image.

■ Elements posterizes the
image.

5 Click **OK**.

■ Elements applies the
changes.

139

USING THE THRESHOLD COMMAND

You can use the
Threshold command
to convert color or
grayscale images into
black-and-white images.
Colors convert to either
black or white depending
on the threshold you set.

If you make a selection
before performing the
Threshold command, you
only affect the selected
pixels. Similarly, if you have
a multilayered image, your
adjustments only affect the
selected layer. See Chapter
4 to make a selection and
Chapter 9 for more on
layers.

USING THE THRESHOLD COMMAND

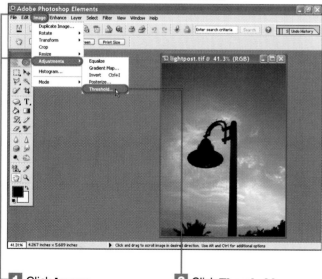

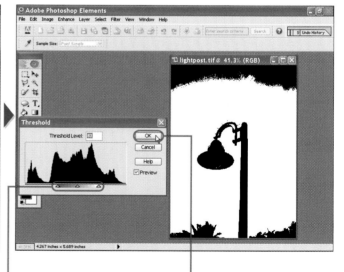

1 Click **Image**.

2 Click **Adjustments**.

3 Click **Threshold**.

■ The Threshold dialog box
appears.

4 Click and drag the slider
(⬛) to set a threshold
between 1 and 255.

■ Elements converts the
image to black and white.

5 Click **OK**.

■ Elements applies the
changes.

You can use the Adjustment Invert command to invert all the colors in a photograph, converting it to a photographic negative. If you have a photographic negative to begin with, inverting changes it into a positive.

If you make a selection before performing the Invert command, you only affect the selected pixels. Similarly, if you have a multilayered image, your adjustments only affect the selected layer. See Chapter 4 to make a selection and Chapter 9 for more on layers.

INVERT THE COLORS OF AN IMAGE

1 Click **Image**.

2 Click **Adjustments**.

3 Click **Invert**.

■ Elements inverts the colors in the image.

CHAPTER 8

Retouching Photographs

Do you want to improve the quality of your digital photographs by adjusting their exposure or removing unwanted objects or blemishes? Elements provides a variety of tools and commands to fix photographs quickly and easily.

APPLY A QUICK FIX

You can apply a variety of common retouching commands — such as adjusting brightness and focus — using the Quick Fix feature. The Quick Fix dialog box lets you preview the results before applying the commands to your image.

Some of the commands available through the Quick Fix dialog box are covered in more detail in this chapter and in Chapter 7.

If you make a selection before performing the Quick Fix command, changes only affect the selected pixels. See Chapter 4 for more on making selections.

APPLY A QUICK FIX

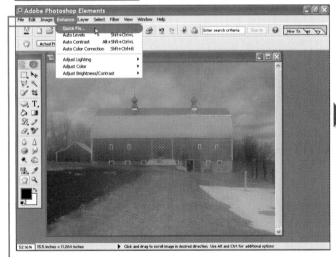

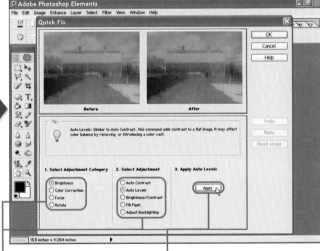

1 Click **Enhance**.

2 Click **Quick Fix**.

■ The Quick Fix dialog box opens.

3 Click an adjustment category (○ changes to ◉).

4 Click an adjustment (○ changes to ◉).

■ In this example, Auto Levels is applied to improve brightness and contrast.

5 Click **Apply**.

How do I undo adjustments that I have made in the Quick Fix dialog box?

You can click **Undo** to undo the most recent Quick Fix adjustment. Clicking **Undo** multiple times will undo multiple adjustments, if you have made them. You can redo an adjustment that was just undone by clicking the **Redo** button. Clicking **Reset Image** reverts the image to the state it was in when you opened the Quick Fix dialog box.

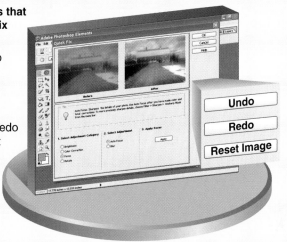

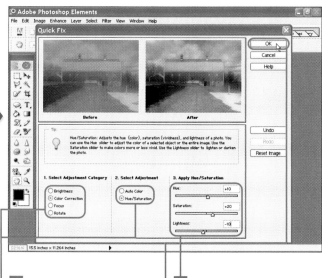

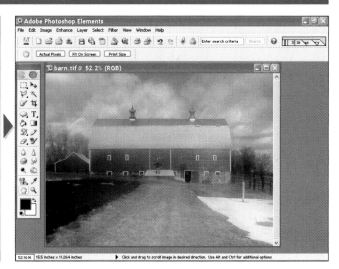

6 Click another adjustment category (○ changes to ◉).

7 Click another adjustment (○ changes to ◉).

■ In this example, Hue and Saturation are adjusted to improve color.

8 Specify your adjustment settings by clicking and dragging a ⌂.

■ You can continue to make more adjustments from other categories.

9 Click **OK**.

■ Elements applies the Quick Fix adjustments to your image.

USING THE CLONE STAMP

You can clean up small flaws or erase elements in your image with the Clone Stamp tool. The tool copies information from one area of an image to another.

USING THE CLONE STAMP

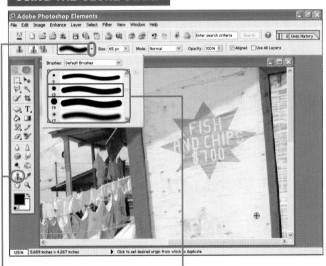

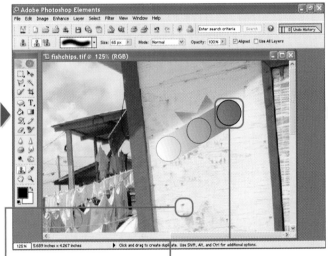

1 Click the Clone Stamp tool ([image]).

2 Click the Brush [·].

3 Select a brush size and type.

4 Press and hold Alt (option) and click the area of the image from which you want to copy.

■ In this example, an empty area on the side of a building is selected.

5 Release the Alt (option) key.

6 Click and drag your cursor (○) inside the selection to apply the clone stamp.

How can I make the clone stamp's effects look seamless?

To erase elements from your image with the rubber stamp without leaving a trace, try the following:

- Clone between areas of similar color and texture.

- To apply the rubber stamp more subtly, lower its opacity.

- Use a soft-edged brush shape.

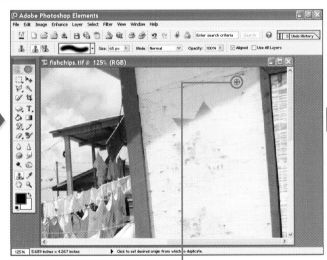

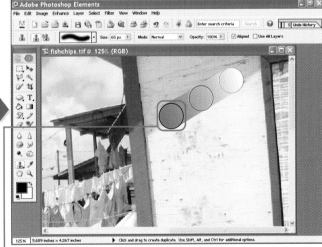

■ Elements copies the selected area to where you click and drag.

7 To copy another part of your image, press and hold **Alt** (**option**) and click another area.

8 Release the **Alt** (**option**) key.

9 Click and drag your cursor (◯) within the selection to copy the newly selected area.

■ This example erases the painted information on the side of the building by copying from the surrounding area.

USING THE RED EYE BRUSH

You can use the Red Eye Brush to remove the reddish eye color that a camera flash can cause.

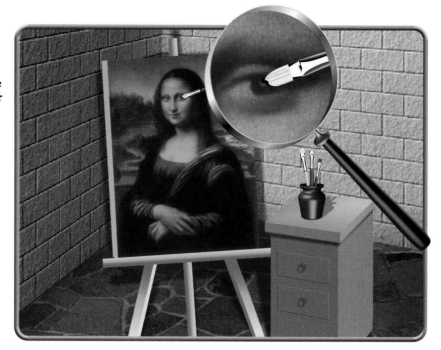

USING THE RED EYE BRUSH

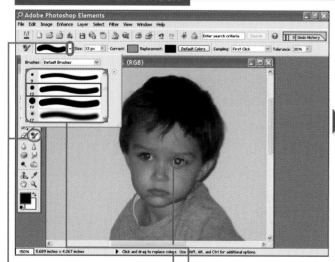

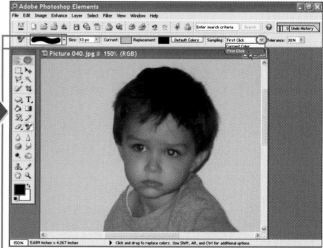

1 Click the Red Eye Brush ().

2 Click ⊡.

3 Click a brush that covers each eye in your image.

■ You can hold the circular brush over an eye to match the brush to the eye size.

4 Click ⌄ (⊡).

5 Click **First Click**, which replaces the eye color you click in the image.

■ You can click **Current Color** to replace the color in the Current box instead.

Why might I want to choose colors for the Red Eye Brush other than the default colors?

For eyes, the default settings will probably suffice. But if you use the brush to fix other elements in your image, you may want to adjust the colors. For example, you may want to specify the replacement color as white when getting rid of braces on teeth.

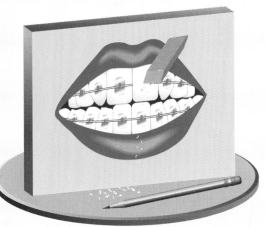

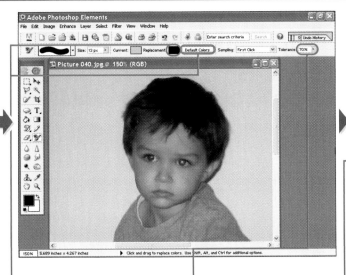

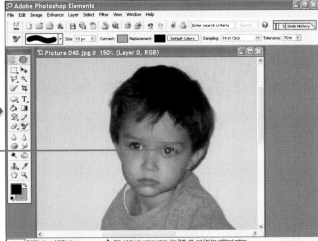

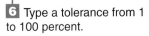

■ You can click the Replacement box (■) to specify a replacement color other than black, the default.

■ You can click **Default Colors** to reset the Current and Replacement colors to red and black.

6 Type a tolerance from 1 to 100 percent.

■ The higher the tolerance, the more red the brush removes.

7 Click a red eye.

■ Elements replaces the red with the replacement color.

ADJUST BACKLIGHTING

You can adjust the backlighting in an image to reduce the brightness that the sun causes in the background and to bring out some of the background details.

If you make a selection before performing the Adjust Backlighting command, changes only affect the selected pixels. Similarly, if you have a multilayered image, your adjustments only affect the selected layer. See Chapter 4 to make a selection and Chapter 9 for more on layers.

ADJUST BACKLIGHTING

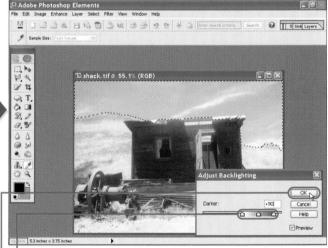

1 Select the backlit area that you want to adjust.

Note: See Chapter 4 for more on making selections.

2 Click **Enhance**.

3 Click **Adjust Lighting**.

4 Click **Adjust Backlighting**.

■ The Adjust Backlighting dialog box appears.

5 Click and drag the Darker slider (△) to darken the backlighting.

6 Click **OK**.

■ Elements decreases the backlighting.

■ To make more precise lighting adjustments, you can use the Levels command as covered in Chapter 7.

ADD FILL FLASH

You can lighten the shadows in a photo using the Fill Flash command. This can help bring out details that might otherwise be hidden.

If you make a selection before performing the Fill Flash command, changes only affect the selected pixels. Similarly, if you have a multilayered image, your adjustments only affect the selected layer. See Chapter 4 to make a selection and Chapter 9 for more on layers.

ADD FILL FLASH

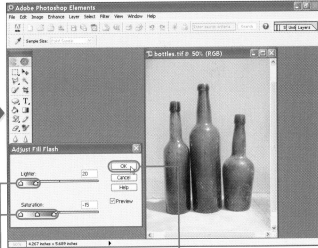

1 Click **Enhance**.

2 Click **Adjust Lighting**.

3 Click **Fill Flash**.

■ The Adjust Fill Flash dialog box appears.

4 Click and drag the Lighter slider ( ) to lighten the image.

5 Click and drag the Saturation slider ( ) to control the color intensity in the lightened image.

6 Click **OK**.

■ Elements lightens the image.

REMOVE A COLOR CAST

You can use the Color Cast command to remove shading affecting your entire image. This command can help remove colors that scanning introduces.

If you make a selection before performing the Color Cast command, you only affect the selected pixels. Similarly, if you have a multilayered image, your adjustments only affect the selected layer. See Chapter 4 to make a selection and Chapter 9 for more on layers.

REMOVE A COLOR CAST

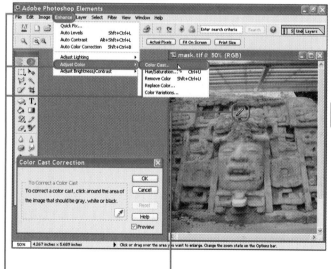

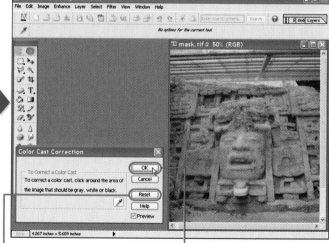

1 Click **Enhance**.

2 Click **Adjust Color**.

3 Click **Color Cast**.

■ The Color Cast Correction dialog box opens.

4 Click a part of your image that the casted color affects.

■ Elements removes the color cast across the entire image.

■ You can click **Reset** to undo the command and try again.

5 Click **OK**.

■ Elements applies the change.

REMOVE DUST AND SCRATCHES

You can add slight blurring to your image to remove extraneous dust and scratches with the Dust & Scratches filter. This can help improve scans of old photographs.

REMOVE DUST AND SCRATCHES

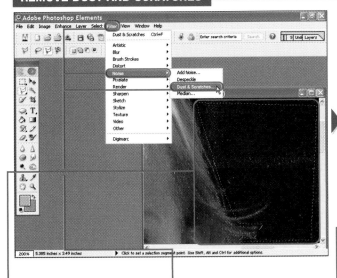

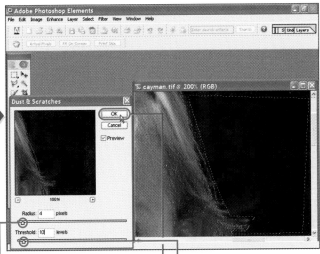

1 Select an area that has dust and scratches with a selection tool.

Note: For more about making selections, see Chapter 4.

2 Click **Filter**.

3 Click **Noise**.

4 Click **Dust & Scratches**.

■ The Dust & Scratches dialog box appears.

5 Click and drag the Radius slider (△) to control what size speck to consider dust or a scratch.

6 Click and drag the Threshold slider (△) to control how much pixels need to differ from their surroundings to be considered dust or a scratch.

7 Click **OK**.

■ Elements applies the filter.

CHAPTER 9

Working with Layers

Do you want to separate the elements in your image so that you can move and transform them independently of one another? You can do this by placing them in different layers.

WHAT ARE LAYERS?

A Photoshop Elements image can consist of multiple layers, with each layer containing different objects in the image.

Layer Independence

Layered Elements files act like several images combined into one. Each layer of an image has its own set of pixels that you can move and transform independently of the pixels in other layers.

Apply Commands to Layers

Most Elements commands affect only the layer that you select. For example, if you click and drag using the Move tool, the selected layer moves while the other layers stay in place; if you apply a color adjustment, only colors in the selected layer change.

Manipulate Layers

You can combine, duplicate, and hide layers in an image. You can also shuffle the order in which you stack layers. You perform most of these actions using the Layers palette.

Transparency

Layers can have transparent areas, where the elements on the layers below can show through. When you perform a cut or erase command on a layer, the affected pixels become transparent. Layers can also have semitransparent areas where objects below can only partially show through.

Adjustment Layers

Adjustment layers are special layers that contain information about color or tonal adjustments. An adjustment layer affects the pixels in all the layers below it. You can increase or decrease an adjustment layer's strength to get precisely the effect you want.

Save Layered Files

You can only save multilayered images in the Photoshop, Photoshop PDF, and TIFF file formats. To save a layered image in another file format — for example, BMP, GIF, or JPEG — you must combine the image's layers into a single layer, a process known as *flattening*. For more information about saving files, see Chapter 14.

CREATE AND ADD TO A LAYER

To keep elements in your image independent from one another, you can create separate layers and add objects to them.

CREATE A LAYER

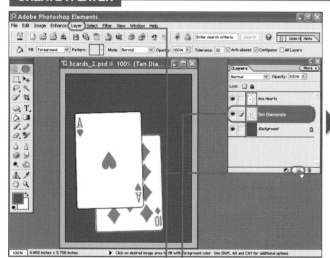

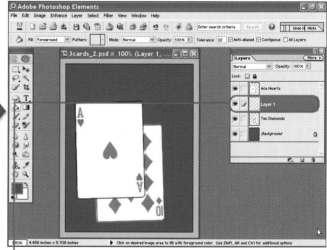

1 Open the Layers palette.

Note: For more information on opening and using palettes, see Chapter 1.

2 Click the layer above which you want to add the new layer.

3 In the Layers palette, click the New Layer button (⬚).

■ Alternatively, you can click **Layer**, **New**, and then **Layer**.

■ Elements creates a new, transparent layer.

Note: To change the name of a layer, see the section "Rename a Layer."

What is the Background layer?

The Background layer is the default bottom layer that appears when you create a new image or when you import an image from a scanner or digital camera. You can create new layers on top of a Background layer, but not below it. Unlike other layers, a Background layer cannot contain transparent pixels.

ADD TO A LAYER

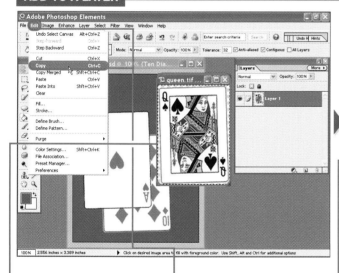

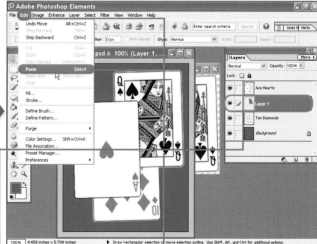

■ This example shows adding content to the new layer by copying and pasting from another image file.

1 Open another image.

2 Using a selection tool, select the content you want to copy in the other image.

Note: See Chapter 1 to learn more about opening an image. See Chapter 4 to learn more about the selection tools.

3 Click **Edit**.

4 Click **Copy**.

5 Click the image window where you created the new layer.

6 Click the new layer in the Layers palette.

7 Click **Edit**.

8 Click **Paste**.

■ The content from the other image pastes into the new layer.

HIDE A LAYER

You can hide a layer to temporarily remove elements in that layer from view.

Hidden layers do not display when you print or use the Save for Web command.

HIDE A LAYER

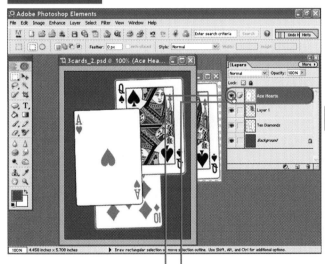

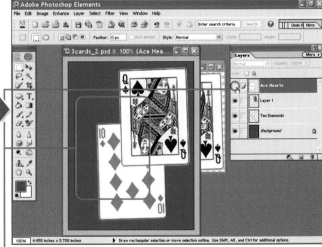

1 Open the Layers palette.

Note: For more about opening and using palettes, see Chapter 1.

2 Click a layer.

3 Click the Eye icon (👁) for the layer.

■ Elements hides the layer and 👁 disappears.

■ To show one layer and hide all the others, you can press Alt (option) and click the 👁 for the layer.

Note: You can also delete a layer. See the section "Delete a Layer" for more information.

MOVE A LAYER

You can use the Move
tool to reposition the
elements in one
layer without
moving those
in others.

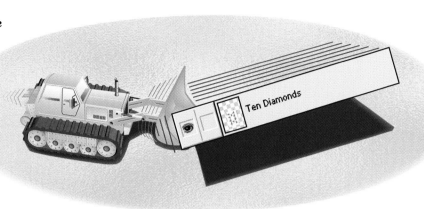

MOVE A LAYER

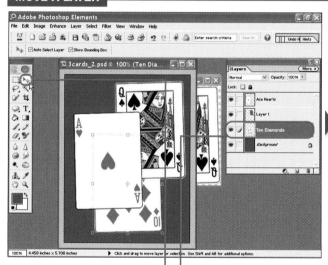 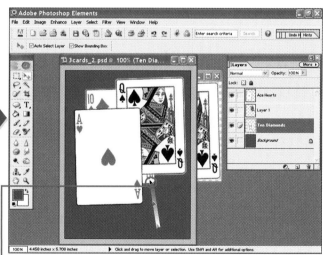

1 Open the Layers
palette.

*Note: For more about opening and
using palettes, see Chapter 1.*

2 Click a layer.

3 Click the Move tool (⊕).

4 Click and drag your
cursor (▶) inside the
window.

■ Content in the selected
layer moves.

■ Content in the other layers
does not move.

*Note: To move several layers at
once, see the section "Link Layers."*

DUPLICATE A LAYER

By duplicating a layer, you can manipulate elements in an image while keeping a copy of their original state.

DUPLICATE A LAYER

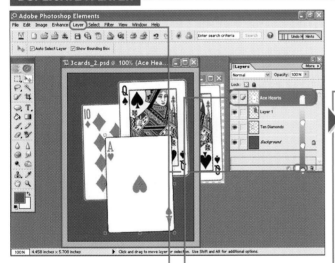

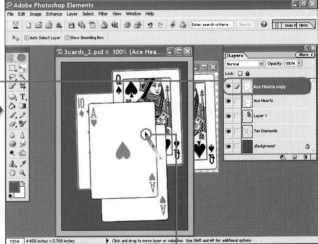

1 Open the Layers palette.

Note: For more about opening and using palettes, see Chapter 1.

2 Click a layer.

3 Click and drag the layer to 🗋.

■ Alternatively, you can click **Layer** and then **Duplicate Layer**, in which case a dialog box appears allowing you to name the layer.

■ Elements duplicates the selected layer.

■ You can see that Elements has duplicated the layer by selecting the new layer, clicking ⊕, and clicking and dragging the layer.

You can delete a layer
when you no longer have
a use for its contents.

Queen Spades

DELETE A LAYER

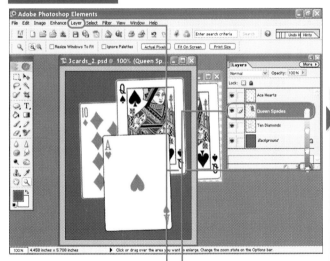

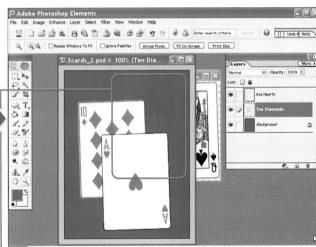

1 Open the Layers
palette.

*Note: For more about opening and
using palettes, see Chapter 1.*

2 Click a layer.

3 Click and drag the layer
to 🗑️.

■ Alternatively, you can click
Layer and then **Delete
Layer**, in which case a
confirmation dialog box
appears.

■ Elements deletes the
selected layer and the
content in the layer
disappears from the
image window.

*Note: You can also hide a layer. See
the section "Hide a Layer" for more
information.*

REORDER LAYERS

You can change the stacking order of layers to move elements forward or backward in your image.

REORDER LAYERS

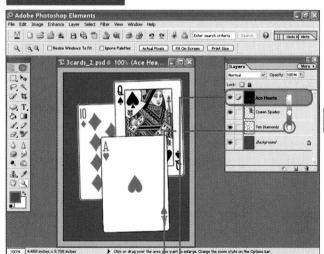

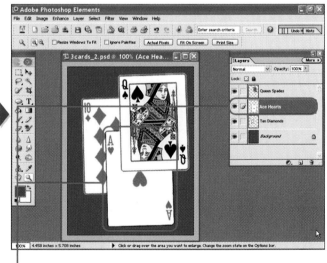

USING THE LAYERS PALETTE

1 Open the Layers palette.

Note: For more about opening and using palettes, see Chapter 1.

2 Click a layer.

3 Click and drag the layer to change its arrangement in the stack.

■ The layer assumes its new position in the stack.

Are there shortcuts for changing the order of layers?

TO MOVE A LAYER	ON A PC PRESS	ON A MAC PRESS
One level up in the stack	Ctrl +]	⌘ +]
One level back in the stack	Ctrl + [	⌘ + [
To the very front of the stack	Shift + Ctrl +]	Shift + ⌘ +]
To the very back of the stack	Shift + Ctrl + [	Shift + ⌘ + [

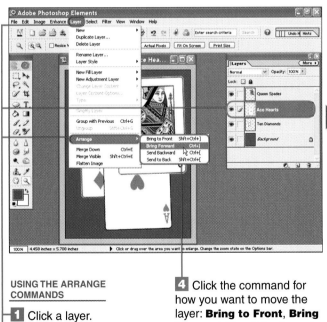

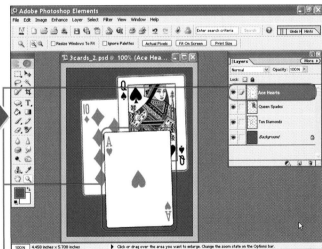

USING THE ARRANGE COMMANDS

■1 Click a layer.

■2 Click **Layer**.

■3 Click **Arrange**.

■4 Click the command for how you want to move the layer: **Bring to Front**, **Bring Forward**, **Send Backward**, or **Send to Back**.

■ The layer assumes its new position in the stack.

Note: You cannot move a layer in back of the default Background layer.

CHANGE THE OPACITY OF A LAYER

Adjusting the opacity of a layer can let elements in the layers below show through. *Opacity* is the opposite of transparency. Decreasing the opacity of a layer increases its transparency.

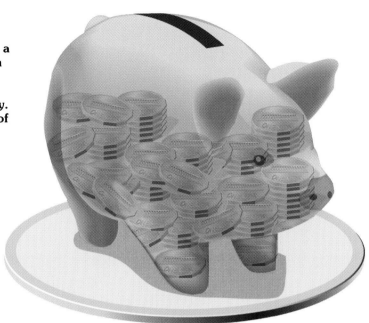

CHANGE THE OPACITY OF A LAYER

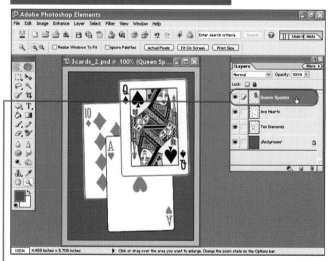

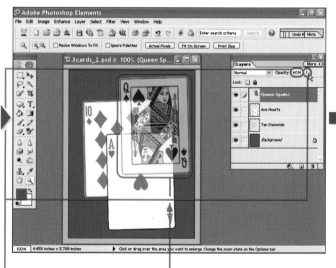

1 Open the Layers palette.

Note: For more about opening and using palettes, see Chapter 1.

2 Click a layer other than the Background layer.

Note: You cannot change the opacity of the Background layer.

■ The default opacity is 100%, which is completely opaque.

3 Type a new value in the Opacity field.

■ Alternatively, you can click and drag the slider.

■ A layer's opacity can range from 0% to 100%.

■ The layer changes in opacity.

How can I use changes in opacity in my layers?

You can lower the opacity to add interesting type effects. For example, you can add a layer of semitransparent type over an image by reducing the type layer's opacity to 50%. For more about adding type, see Chapter 12.

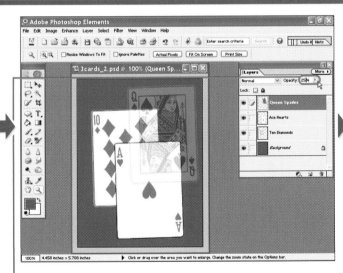

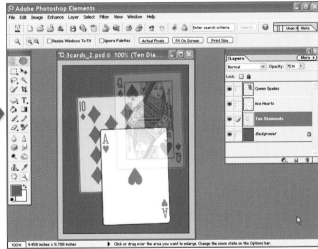

■ You can continue to adjust the opacity to suit your tastes.

■ You can make multiple layers in your image semitransparent by changing their opacities.

■ In this example, both the Queen of Spades and Ten of Diamonds layers are semitransparent.

MERGE AND FLATTEN LAYERS

Merging layers lets you permanently combine information from two or more separate layers. Flattening layers combines all the layers of an image into one.

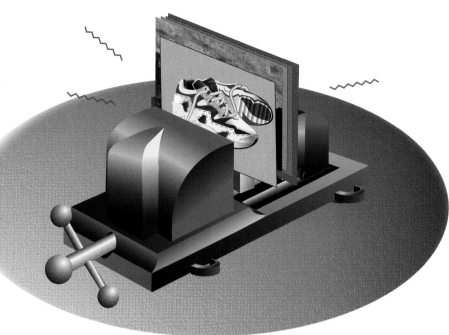

MERGE LAYERS

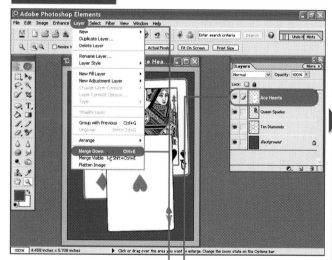
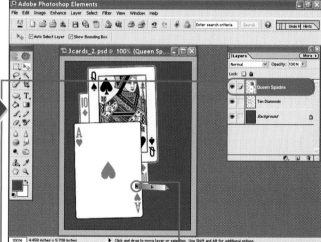

1 Open the Layers palette.

2 Place the two layers you want to merge next to each other.

Note: To use palettes, see Chapter 1. See the section "Reorder Layers" to change stacking order.

3 Click the topmost of the two layers.

4 Click **Layer**.

5 Click **Merge Down**.

■ The two layers merge.

■ Elements keeps the name of the lower layer.

■ To see the result of the merge, select the new layer, click ▶⊕, and click and drag the merged layer.

■ The elements that were previously in separate layers now move together.

168

Why would I want to merge layers?

Merging layers enables you to save computer memory. The fewer layers an Elements image has, the less space it takes up in RAM and on your hard drive when you save it. Merging layers also lets you permanently combine elements of your image when you are happy with how you have arranged them relative to one another. If you want the option of rearranging all the original layers in the future, save a copy of your image before you merge layers.

FLATTEN LAYERS

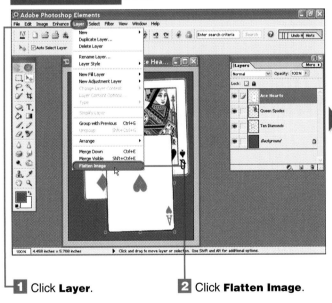

1 Click **Layer**.

2 Click **Flatten Image**.

■ All the layers merge into a single Background layer.

RENAME A LAYER

You can rename a layer to give it a name that best describes its content.

RENAME A LAYER

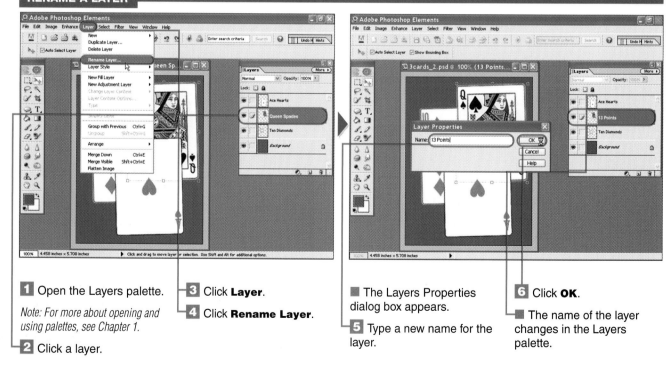

1 Open the Layers palette.

Note: For more about opening and using palettes, see Chapter 1.

2 Click a layer.

3 Click **Layer**.

4 Click **Rename Layer**.

■ The Layers Properties dialog box appears.

5 Type a new name for the layer.

6 Click **OK**.

■ The name of the layer changes in the Layers palette.

You can use a Transform tool to change the shape of the objects in a layer. Transforming just a layer allows you to keep the rest of your image unchanged.

TRANSFORM A LAYER

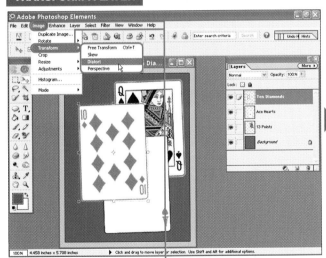

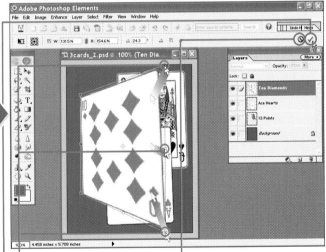

1 Open the Layers palette.

Note: For more about opening and using palettes, see Chapter 1.

2 Click **Image**.

3 Click **Transform**.

4 Click a Transform tool.

5 Click and drag the side and corner handles (■) to transform the shape of the layer.

6 Click ✓ or press **Enter** (**Return**) to commit the change.

■ You can click ◯ or press **Esc** (⌘ + .) to cancel the change.

Note: For more about transforming your images, see Chapter 5.

171

CREATE A SOLID FILL LAYER

You can create a solid fill layer to place an opaque layer of color throughout your image.

CREATE A SOLID FILL LAYER

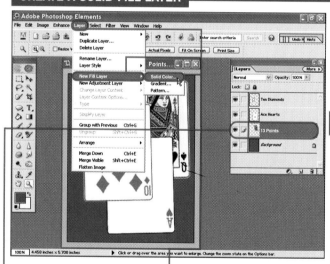

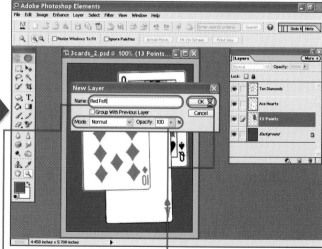

1 Open the Layers palette.

Note: For more about opening and using palettes, see Chapter 1.

2 Click the layer above which you want to add solid color.

3 Click **Layer**.

4 Click **New Fill Layer**.

5 Click **Solid Color**.

■ The New Layer dialog box appears.

6 Type a name for the layer.

■ You can specify a type of blend or opacity setting for the layer.

Note: See "Blend Layers" or "Change the Opacity of a Layer" for details.

7 Click **OK**.

How do I add solid color to just part of a solid fill layer?

Make a selection with a selection tool before creating the solid fill layer. Elements only adds color inside the selection. See Chapter 4 for more about making selections.

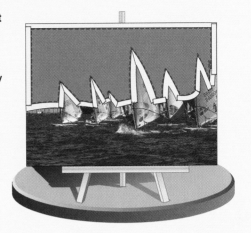

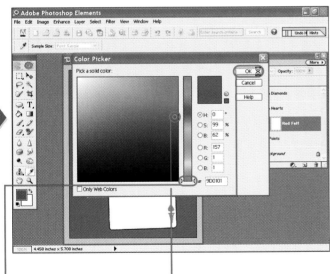

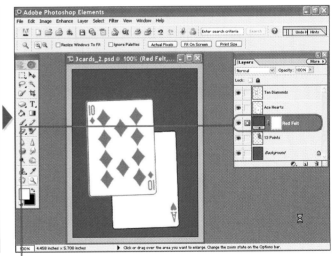

■ The Color Picker dialog box appears.

8 To change the range of colors that appears in the window, click and drag the slider (◁).

9 Select a fill color by clicking your cursor (○) in the color window.

10 Click **OK**.

■ Elements creates a new layer filled with a solid color.

■ Layers above the new layer are not affected.

CREATE A GRADIENT FILL LAYER

You can create a gradient fill layer to place color transition throughout your image.

CREATE A GRADIENT FILL LAYER

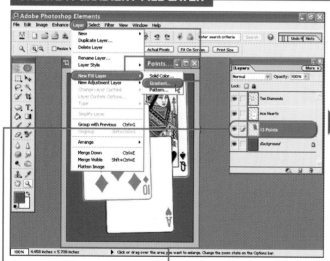

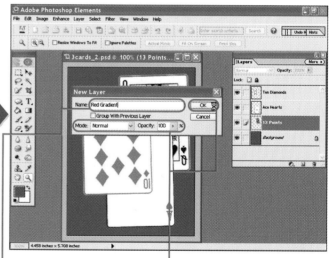

1 Open the Layers palette.

Note: For more about opening and using palettes, see Chapter 1.

2 Click the layer above which you want to add a gradient.

3 Click **Layer**.

4 Click **New Fill Layer**.

5 Click **Gradient**.

■ The New Layer dialog box appears.

6 Type a name for the layer.

■ You can specify a type of blend or opacity setting for the layer.

Note: See the section "Blend Layers" or "Change the Opacity of a Layer" for details.

7 Click **OK**.

How can I convert one type of fill layer to another?

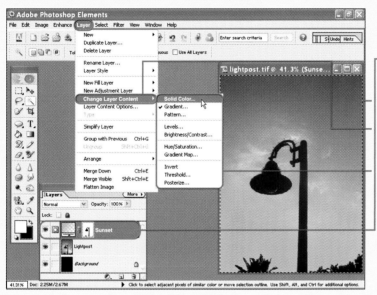

1 Click the layer in the Layers palette.

2 Click **Layer**.

3 Click **Change Layer Content**.

4 Click a different layer type.

■ Elements opens a dialog box that lets you define the new fill layer.

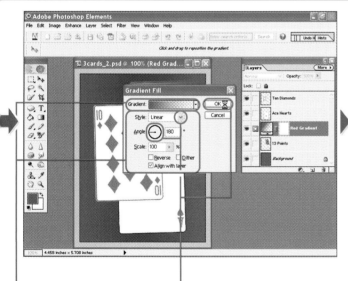

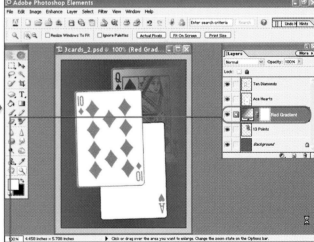

■ The Gradient Fill dialog box appears.

8 Click ☑ (▼) and click a set of gradient colors.

9 Type or click (☐ changes to ☑) to change your other gradient settings.

■ You can click here to select a style that specifies the shape.

■ You can click and drag here to select an angle that specifies the direction.

10 Click **OK**.

■ Elements creates a new layer filled with the specified gradient.

■ Layers above the new layer are not affected.

CREATE A PATTERN FILL LAYER

You can create a pattern fill layer to place repeating designs throughout your image.

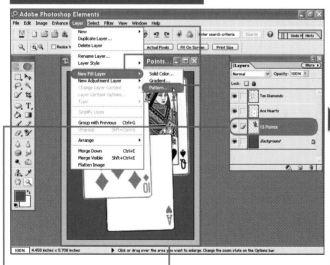

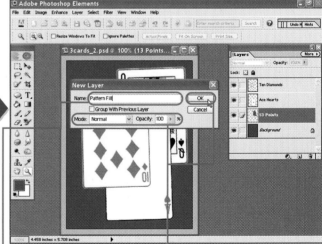

1 Open the Layers palette.

Note: For more about opening and using palettes, see Chapter 1.

2 Click the layer above which you want to add a pattern.

3 Click **Layer**.

4 Click **New Fill Layer**.

5 Click **Pattern**.

■ The New Layer dialog box appears.

6 Type a name for the layer.

■ You can specify a type of blend or opacity setting for the layer.

Note: See "Blend Layers" or "Change the Opacity of a Layer" for details.

7 Click **OK**.

How do I change the applied pattern after creating a pattern fill layer?

Double-click the layer thumbnail in the Layers palette. The Pattern Fill dialog box appears and enables you to edit the pattern.

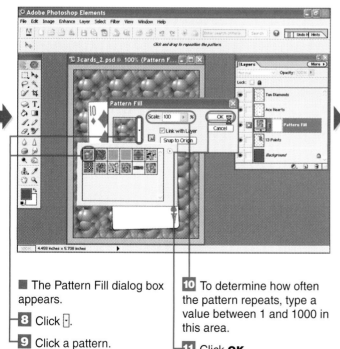

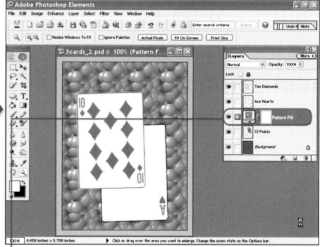

■ The Pattern Fill dialog box appears.

8 Click ⊡.

9 Click a pattern.

10 To determine how often the pattern repeats, type a value between 1 and 1000 in this area.

11 Click **OK**.

■ Elements creates a new layer filled with a pattern.

■ Layers above the new layer are not affected.

Note: For more information about patterns, see "Using the Pattern Stamp" in Chapter 6.

CREATE AN ADJUSTMENT LAYER

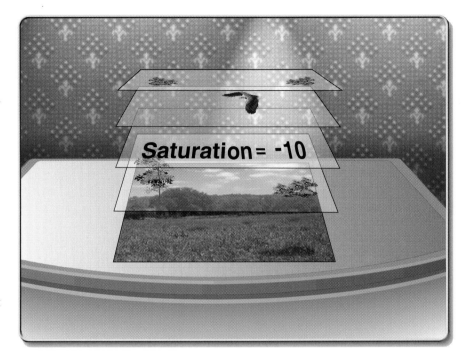

Adjustment layers let you store color and tonal changes in a layer, rather than having them permanently applied to your image. An adjustment layer affects the layers below it.

Saturation = -10

For more information about applying color and tonal adjustments to your image, see Chapter 7.

CREATE AN ADJUSTMENT LAYER

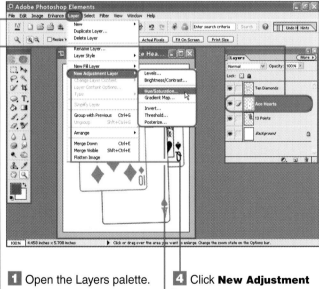

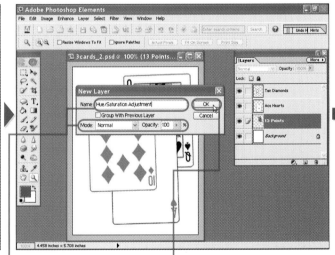

1 Open the Layers palette.

Note: For more about opening and using palettes, see Chapter 1.

2 Click a layer.

3 Click **Layer**.

4 Click **New Adjustment Layer**.

5 Click an adjustment command.

■ The New Layer dialog box appears.

6 Type a name for the adjustment layer.

■ You can specify a type of blend or opacity setting for the layer.

Note: See the section "Blend Layers" or "Change the Opacity of a Layer" for details.

7 Click **OK**.

■ Elements places the new adjustment layer above the currently selected layer.

How do I apply an adjustment layer to only part of my image canvas?

Make a selection with a selection tool before creating the adjustment layer. See Chapter 4 for more about making selections.

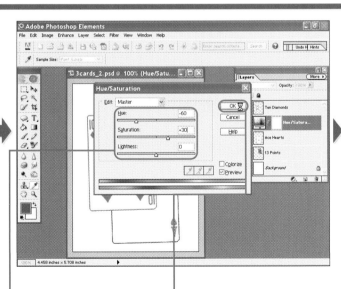

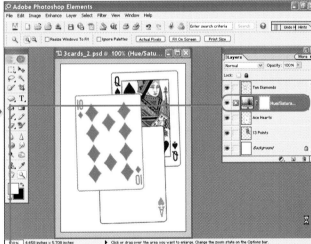

■ The dialog box for the adjustment command appears.

8 Click and drag the sliders (⌂) and type values to adjust the settings.

■ In this example, an adjustment layer is created that changes the hue and saturation.

9 Click **OK**.

■ Elements adds an adjustment layer to the image.

■ Elements applies the effect to the layers that are below the adjustment layer.

■ In this example, Elements affects the card layers below the adjustment layer while leaving the card layer above it unaffected.

EDIT AN ADJUSTMENT LAYER

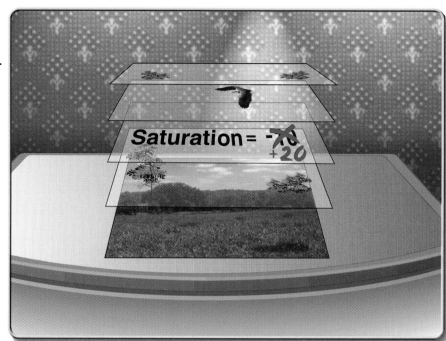

You can change the color and tonal changes that you defined in an adjustment layer. This lets you fine-tune your adjustment layer to get the effect you want.

EDIT AN ADJUSTMENT LAYER

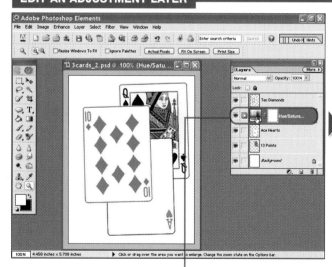

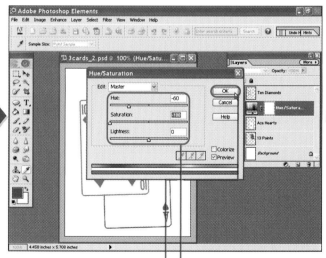

1 Open the Layers palette.

Note: For more about opening and using palettes, see Chapter 1.

2 Double-click the adjustment layer in the Layers palette.

■ The settings dialog box corresponding to the adjustment command appears.

3 Click and drag the sliders (△) to change the settings in the dialog box.

4 Click **OK**.

How do I merge an adjustment layer with a regular layer?

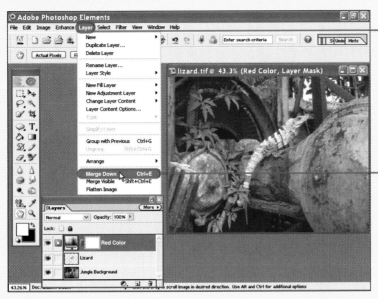

1 Place the adjustment layer over the layer with which you want to merge it.

Note: See the section "Reorder Layers" for more information.

2 Click **Layer**.

3 Click **Merge Down**.

■ When you merge the layers, Elements only applies the adjustment layer's effects to the layer with which you merged.

■ In this example, only the lizard layer remains tinted red after the merge.

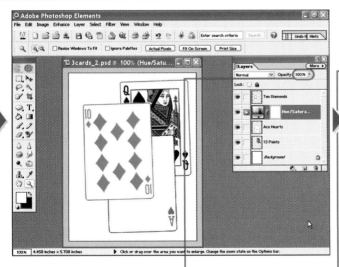

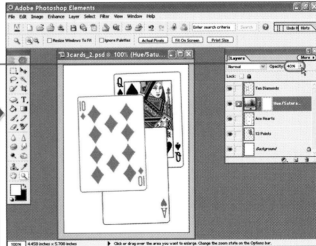

■ Elements applies your changes.

■ In this example, the saturation was reduced to the minimum, which removed the color in the layers below the adjustment layer.

■ You can lessen the effect of an adjustment layer by typing a value to decrease the layer's opacity to less than 100%.

■ In this example, the opacity was decreased to 40%, which reverses the decrease in saturation. Some of the original color in the cards returns.

LINK LAYERS

Linking causes different layers to move in unison when you move them with the Move tool. You may find linking useful when you want to keep elements of an image aligned with one another, but do not want to merge their layers. Keeping layers unmerged lets you apply effects independently of each. See the section "Merge and Flatten Layers" for more on merging.

LINK LAYERS

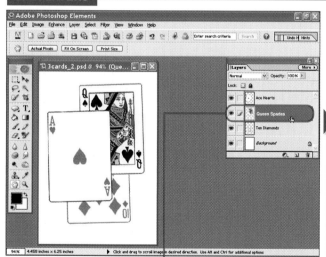

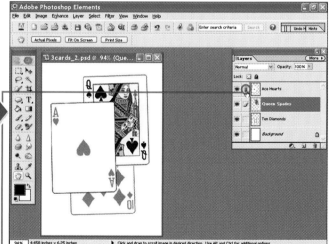

CREATE A LINK

1 Open the Layers palette.

Note: For more about opening and using palettes, see Chapter 1.

2 Click one of the layers you want to link.

3 Click the box next to the other layer that you want to link.

■ Doing so turns on a linking icon (🔗).

■ The layers link together.

How do I keep from changing a layer after I have it the way I want it?

You can lock the layer by clicking the Lock icon (🔒) located on the Layers palette. You cannot move, delete, or otherwise edit a locked layer. You can click the Transparency icon (🔲) if you just want to prevent a user from editing the transparent pixels in the layer.

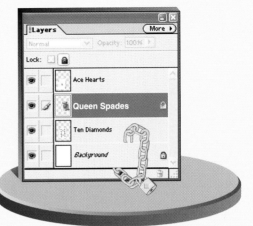

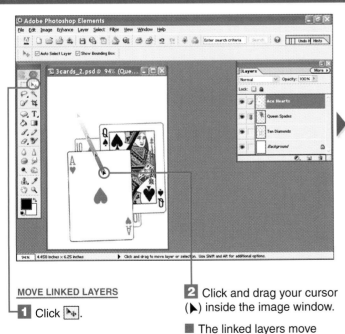

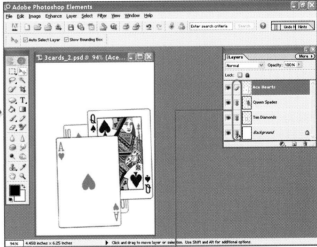

MOVE LINKED LAYERS

1 Click 🔁.

2 Click and drag your cursor (▶) inside the image window.

■ The linked layers move together.

■ You can link as many layers as you like.

■ In this example, all the layers have been linked, including the Background layer.

BLEND LAYERS

You can use Elements' blending modes to specify how pixels in a layer blend with the layers below it. Adjusting blending settings can help you create colorful effects in your layered images.

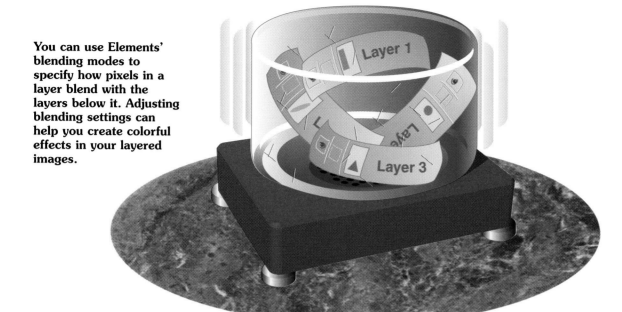

BLEND LAYERS

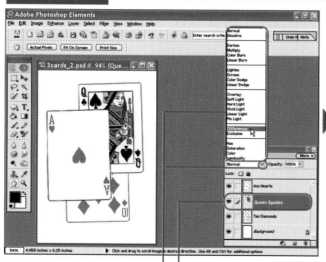

BLEND A REGULAR LAYER

1 Open the Layers palette.

Note: For more about opening and using palettes, see Chapter 1.

2 Click the layer that you want to blend.

3 Click ✓ (⬍).

4 Click a blend mode.

■ Elements blends the selected layer with the layers below it.

■ This example shows the Difference mode, which creates a photonegative effect where the selected layer overlaps other layers, including the Background layer.

184

What effects do some of the different blending modes have?

The Multiply mode darkens the colors where the selected layer overlaps layers below it. The Screen mode is the opposite of Multiply; it lightens colors where layers overlap. Color takes the selected layer's colors and blends them with the details in the layers below it. Luminosity is the opposite of Color; it takes the selected layer's details and mixes them with the colors below it.

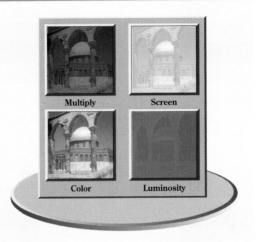

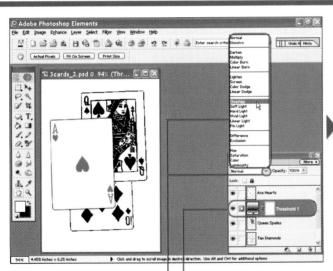

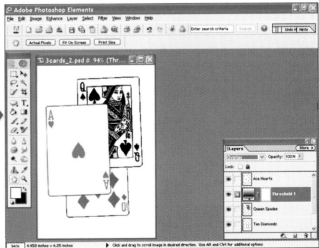

BLEND AN ADJUSTMENT LAYER

1 Open the Layers palette.

Note: For more about opening and using palettes, see Chapter 1.

2 Click an adjustment layer that you want to blend.

3 Click ⌄ (⬍).

4 Click a blend mode.

■ Elements blends the selected layer with the layers below it.

■ This example shows the Overlay mode applied to a Threshold adjustment layer, which lets some of the original color through.

CHAPTER 10

Applying Effects and Styles

You can create special effects for your images by applying Elements' built-in effects. The effects let you add shadows, glows, and 3-D appearances to your art. You can also add special effects to your layers with Elements' layer styles.

ADD A DROP SHADOW TO AN IMAGE

You can apply a drop shadow to make your image look like it is raised off the image canvas.

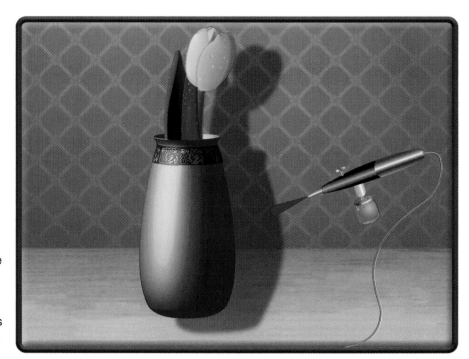

You can also apply a drop shadow to just a layer. See the section "Add a Drop Shadow to a Layer" for more information.

Because this effect flattens the layers in your image, it is best to apply it last.

APPLY A DROP SHADOW TO AN IMAGE

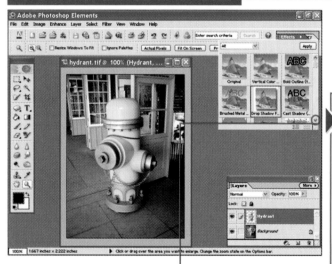

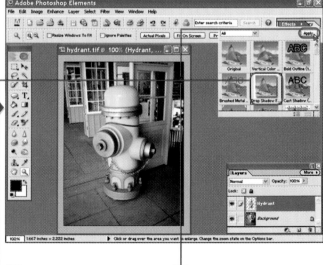

1 Open the Effects palette.

Note: For more information on opening and using palettes, see Chapter 1.

■ You can click ▾ to scroll through the available effects.

2 Click **Drop Shadow Frame**.

3 Click **Apply**.

What other shadow effects are there?

You can make a selection to your image and then click **Cut Out**. This erases the selected pixels and places a shadow along the edge of the cut-out. You can access the Cut Out effect by selecting **Frames** in the menu at the top of the Effects palette. See the section "Frame an Image" for more information about Frame effects.

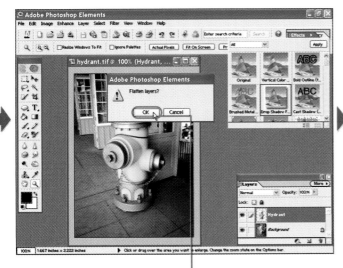

■ If you have a multilayered image, a dialog box appears asking if you want to flatten the layers.

4 Click **OK**.

■ Elements increases the canvas size and places an offset shadow under the image.

FRAME AN IMAGE

You can apply one
of several frame
styles to add a
traditional or flashy
frame around your
image.

Because this effect
flattens the layers in
your image, it is
best to apply it last.

FRAME AN IMAGE

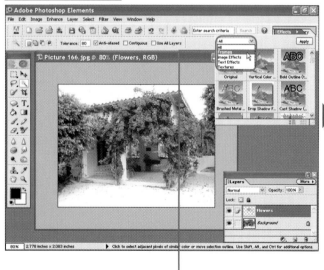

1 Open the Effects
palette.

*Note: For more information on
opening and using palettes, see
Chapter 1.*

2 Click ⌄ (▣) and click
Frames.

3 Click an effect.

■ You can click ⌄ to view
other effects in the palette.

4 Click **Apply**.

What are some of the types of frame effects in Elements?

You can give your art a modern look with a **Brushed Aluminum Frame**, create torn edges around your image with a **Spatter Frame**, or create a custom color border with a **Foreground Color Frame**. Click 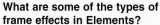 in the Effects palette to see all the frame choices available.

Brushed Aluminum Frame

Spatter Frame

Foreground Color Frame

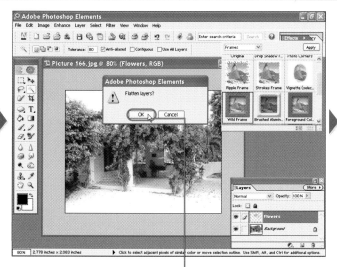

■ If you have a multilayered image, a dialog box appears asking if you want to flatten the layers.

5 Click **OK**.

■ Elements creates a frame around the outer edge of the image.

ADD A FANCY BACKGROUND

You add a fancy
background to your
image with one of
Elements' several
texture effects.

ADD A FANCY BACKGROUND

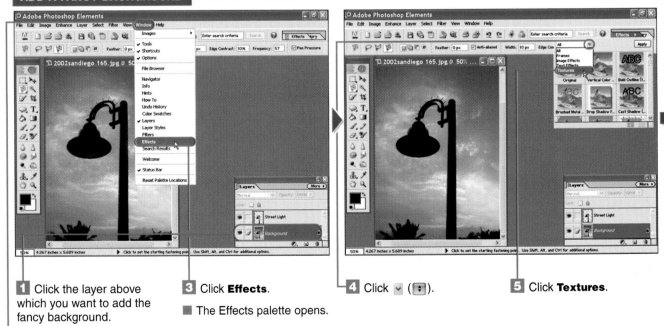

1 Click the layer above
which you want to add the
fancy background.

2 Click **Window**.

3 Click **Effects**.

■ The Effects palette opens.

4 Click ⌄ (⬛).

5 Click **Textures**.

Is there an easy way to preview what each effect will look like?

You can click the List View button (▦) to change how you view the options in the Effects palette. List View displays two generic thumbnails that show how an image appears before and after applying an effect.

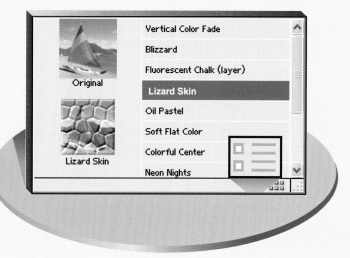

6 Click an effect.

■ You can click ▼ to view other effects in the palette.

7 Click **Apply**.

■ Elements fills the layer with the texture.

ADD A DROP SHADOW TO A LAYER

You can add a drop shadow to a layer to give objects a 3-D look.

ADD A DROP SHADOW TO A LAYER

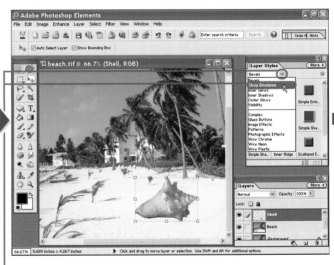

1 Open the Layers palette.

2 Open the Layer Styles palette.

Note: For more information on opening and using palettes, see Chapter 1.

3 Click the layer to which you want to add a drop shadow.

4 Click ☑ (▤) in the Layer Styles palette.

5 Click **Drop Shadows**.

■ Drop shadow styles display.

How do I add an inner shadow to a layer?

An inner shadow creates a "cut out" effect, with the selected layer appearing to drop behind the image canvas. This can have an interesting effect when applied to a layer of type. See Chapter 12 for more about type. To add this effect:

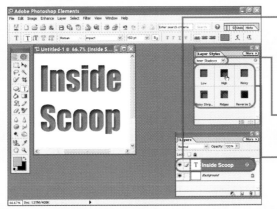

1 Click a layer.

2 Open the Layer Styles palette.

Note: For more information on opening and using palettes, see Chapter 1.

3 Click ✔ ( ) and click **Inner Shadows**.

4 Click an Inner Shadow style.

■ Elements applies the inner shadow.

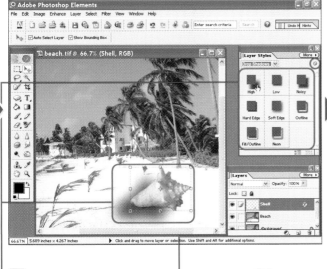

6 Click a drop shadow style.

■ Elements applies the drop shadow to the layer.

■ You can click to remove the drop shadow.

7 Double-click the Style icon ( ) in the affected layer.

■ The Style Settings dialog box opens.

8 Click and drag the Lighting Angle dial to specify the direction of the shadowing.

9 Click and drag ⌂ to increase or decrease the distance of the shadow from your layer.

10 Click **OK**.

■ Elements applies the style settings.

ADD BEVELING TO A LAYER

You can bevel a layer to give objects in your image a three-dimensional look.

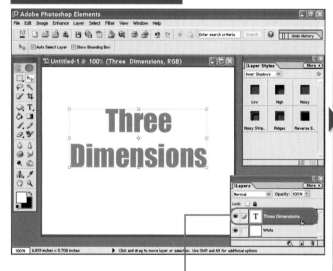

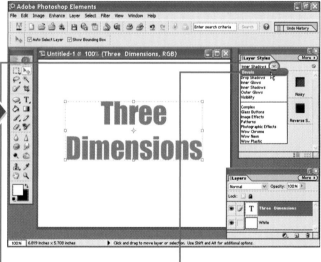

1 Open the Layers palette.

2 Open the Layer Styles palette.

Note: For more information on opening and using palettes, see Chapter 1.

3 Click the layer that you want to bevel.

■ In this example, a type layer is beveled.

Note: For more information about using type, see Chapter 12.

4 Click ✓ (⬍) in the Layer Styles palette.

5 Click **Bevels**.

When would I use the bevel style?

You may find this effect useful for creating three-dimensional buttons for Web pages. For example, to create such a 3-D button, you can apply beveling to a colored rectangle and then lay type over it. See Chapter 6 for details about creating button shapes.

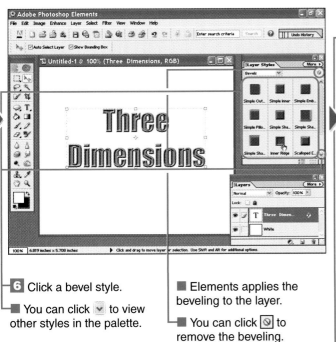

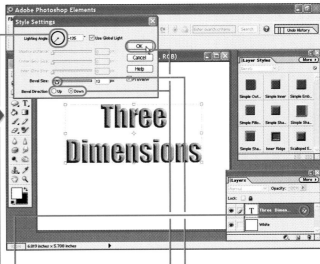

6 Click a bevel style.

■ You can click 🔽 to view other styles in the palette.

■ Elements applies the beveling to the layer.

■ You can click 🚫 to remove the beveling.

7 Double-click 📋 in the affected layer.

■ The Style Settings dialog box opens.

8 Click and drag the Lighting Angle dial to set direction of the beveling.

9 Click and drag 🔺 to increase or decrease the bevel size.

■ You can click here (○ changes to ⦿) to set the bevel direction.

10 Click **OK**.

■ Elements applies the style settings.

ADD AN OUTER GLOW TO A LAYER

The outer glow style adds faint coloring to the outside edge of a layer, which can help highlight it.

ADD AN OUTER GLOW TO A LAYER

1 Open the Layers palette.

2 Open the Layer Styles palette.

Note: For more information on opening and using palettes, see Chapter 1.

3 Click the layer to which you want to add an outer glow.

4 Click ⌄ (▾) in the Layer Styles palette.

5 Click **Outer Glows**.

Can I add an inner glow to layer objects?

Yes. An inner glow adds color to the inside edge of a layer object. To add this effect:

1 Click a layer.

2 Open the Layer Styles palette.

Note: For more information on opening and using palettes, see Chapter 1.

3 Click ▾ (▾) in the Layer Styles palette and click **Inner Glows**.

4 Click an Inner Glow style.

■ Elements applies the inner glow.

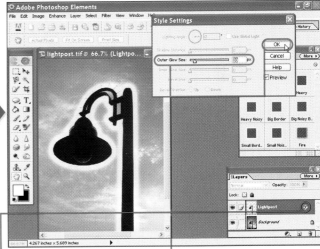

6 Click an outer glow style.

■ You can click ▾ to view other styles in the palette.

■ Elements applies the outer glow to the layer.

■ You can click ⊘ to remove the outer glow.

7 Double-click ▓ in the affected layer.

■ The Style Settings dialog box opens.

8 Click and drag △ to increase or decrease the Outer Glow size.

9 Click **OK**.

■ Elements applies the style settings.

199

ADD A FANCY COVERING TO A LAYER

You can apply any of a variety of layer effects that can make a layer look as if it is covered in colorful metal or glass.

ADD A FANCY COVERING TO A LAYER

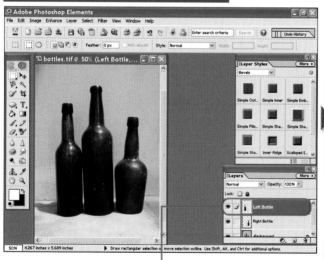

COVER WITH METAL

1 Open the Layers palette.

2 Open the Layer Styles palette.

Note: For more information on opening and using palettes, see Chapter 1.

3 Click the layer that you want to cover.

4 Click ∨ (⬆) in the Layer Styles palette.

5 Click **Wow Chrome**.

Is there another method to change the way styles affect my layers?

You can scale the intensity of applied styles by doing the following:

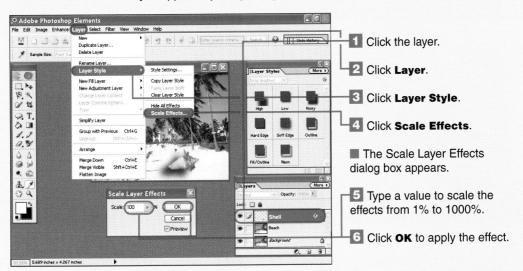

1 Click the layer.

2 Click **Layer**.

3 Click **Layer Style**.

4 Click **Scale Effects**.

■ The Scale Layer Effects dialog box appears.

5 Type a value to scale the effects from 1% to 1000%.

6 Click **OK** to apply the effect.

6 Click a metallic style.

■ Elements applies the style to the layer.

■ You can click ⊘ to remove the outer glow.

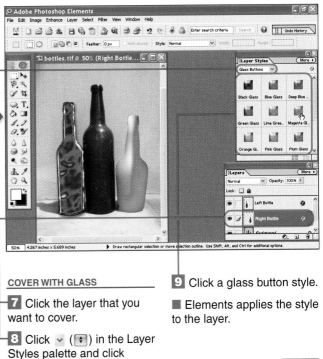

COVER WITH GLASS

7 Click the layer that you want to cover.

8 Click ⌄ (⬥) in the Layer Styles palette and click **Glass Buttons**.

9 Click a glass button style.

■ Elements applies the style to the layer.

CHAPTER 11

Applying Filters

With Elements' filters, you can quickly and easily apply enhancements to your image, including artistic effects, texture effects, and distortions. Filters can help you correct defects in your images or let you turn a photograph into something resembling an impressionist painting. Elements comes with over 100 filters. But this chapter highlights only a few. For details about all the filters, see the Help documentation.

TURN AN IMAGE INTO A PAINTING

You can use many of Elements' artistic filters to make your image look as if you created it with a paintbrush. The Dry Brush filter, for example, applies a painted effect by converting similarly colored areas in your image to solid colors.

To apply the filter to just part of your image, you can make a selection with a selection tool. See Chapter 4 to use selection tools.

TURN AN IMAGE INTO A PAINTING

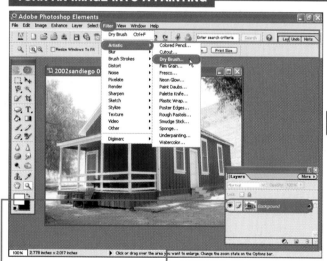

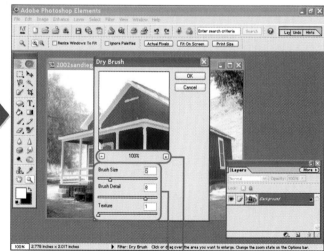

1 Select the layer to which you want to apply the filter.

Note: For more about layers, see Chapter 9.

■ In this example, the image has a single background layer.

2 Click **Filter**.

3 Click **Artistic**.

4 Click **Dry Brush**.

■ The Dry Brush dialog box appears.

■ A small window displays a preview of the filter's effect.

5 Click ⊟ or ⊞ to zoom out or in.

6 Fine-tune the filter effect by typing values for the Brush Size, Brush Detail, and Texture.

What does the Sponge filter do?

The Sponge filter reduces detail and modifies the shapes in an image to create the effect you get when applying a damp sponge to a wet painting. To apply the filter:

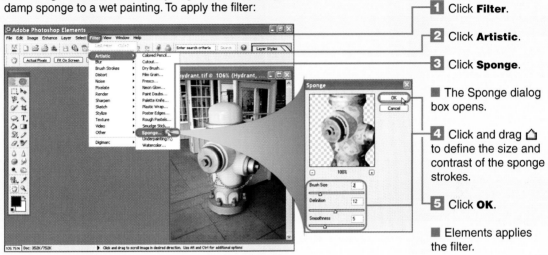

1 Click **Filter**.

2 Click **Artistic**.

3 Click **Sponge**.

■ The Sponge dialog box opens.

4 Click and drag △ to define the size and contrast of the sponge strokes.

5 Click **OK**.

■ Elements applies the filter.

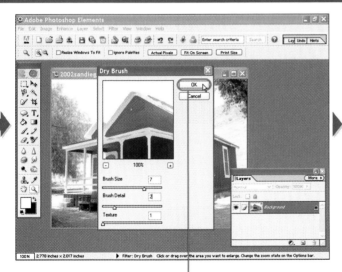

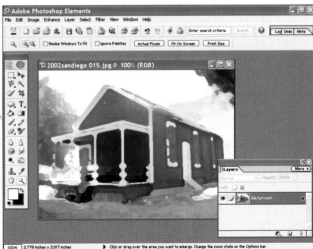

■ This example shows how to thicken the dry-brush effect by increasing Brush Size and decreasing Brush Detail.

7 Click **OK**.

■ Elements applies the filter.

BLUR AN IMAGE

Elements' Blur filters reduce the amount of detail in your image. The Gaussian Blur filter has advantages over the other Blur filters in that you can control the amount of blur that you add.

To apply the filter to just part of your image, you can make a selection with a selection tool. To use the selection tools, see Chapter 4.

BLUR AN IMAGE

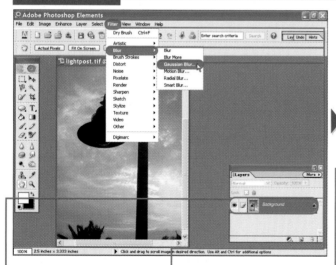

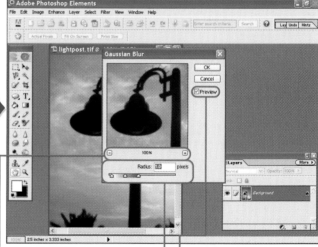

1 Select the layer to which you want to apply the filter.

Note: For more about layers, see Chapter 9.

■ In this example, the image has a single background layer.

2 Click **Filter**.

3 Click **Blur**.

4 Click **Gaussian Blur**.

■ The Gaussian Blur dialog box appears.

■ A small window displays a preview of the filter's effect.

5 Click ⊡ or ⊕ to zoom out or in.

6 Click **Preview** to preview the effect in the main window (☐ changes to ☑).

7 Click and drag the Radius slider (△) to control the amount of blur added.

How do I add directional blurring to an image?

You can add directional blur to objects in your image with the Motion Blur filter, which adds a sense of movement. To apply the filter:

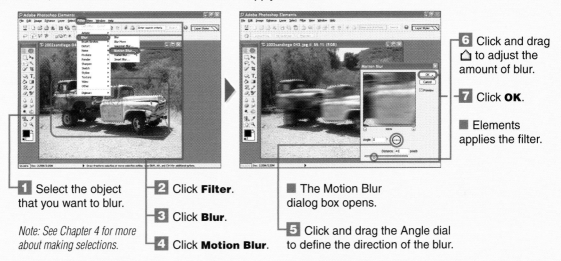

6 Click and drag
⌂ to adjust the
amount of blur.

7 Click **OK**.

■ Elements
applies the filter.

1 Select the object
that you want to blur.

2 Click **Filter**.

3 Click **Blur**.

■ The Motion Blur
dialog box opens.

*Note: See Chapter 4 for more
about making selections.*

4 Click **Motion Blur**.

5 Click and drag the Angle dial
to define the direction of the blur.

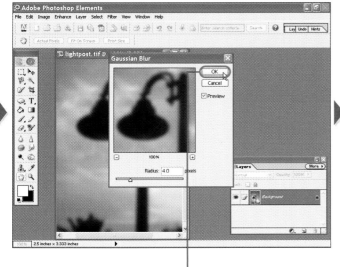

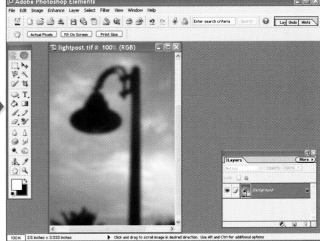

■ In this example, boosting
the Radius value increased
the amount of blur.

8 Click **OK**.

■ Elements applies the filter.

SHARPEN AN IMAGE

Photoshop's Sharpen filters intensify the detail and reduce blurring in your image. The Unsharp Mask filter has advantages over the other Sharpen filters in that it lets you control the amount of sharpening you apply.

To apply the filter to just part of your image, you can make a selection with a selection tool. To use the selection tools, see Chapter 4.

SHARPEN AN IMAGE

1 Select the layer to which you want to apply the filter.

Note: For more about layers, see Chapter 9.

2 Click **Filter**.

3 Click **Sharpen**.

4 Click **Unsharp Mask**.

■ The Unsharp Mask dialog box appears.

■ A small window displays a preview of the filter's effect.

5 Click ▭ or ⊞ to zoom out or in.

6 Click **Preview** to preview the effect in the main window (▯ changes to ☑).

7 Click and drag the sliders (△) to control the amount of sharpening you apply to the image.

When should I apply sharpening?

Sharpening an image after you change its size is a good idea because changing an image's size adds blurring. Applying the Unsharp Mask filter can also help clarify scanned images.

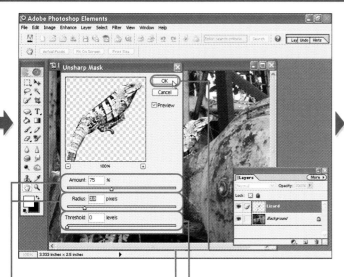

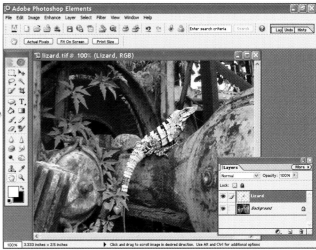

■ **Amount** controls the overall amount of sharpening.

■ **Radius** controls whether sharpening is confined to edges in the image (low Radius setting) or added across the entire image (high Radius setting).

■ **Threshold** controls how much contrast you must have present for an edge to be recognized and sharpened.

8 Click **OK**.

■ Elements applies the filter.

DISTORT AN IMAGE

Elements' Distort filters stretch and squeeze areas of your image. For example, the Spherize filter produces a fun-house mirror effect by making your image look like it is being reflected off a mirrored sphere.

Another way to distort an image is by using the Distort command located under the Image menu. See the section "Skew or Distort a Selection" in Chapter 5 for more information.

To apply the filter to just part of your image, make a selection with a selection tool. See Chapter 4 to use the selection tools.

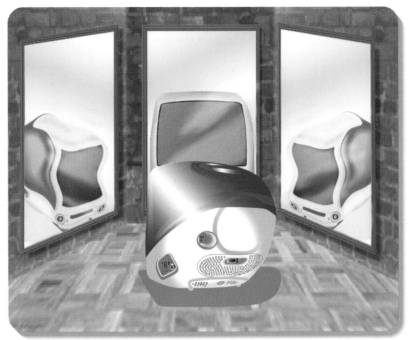

DISTORT AN IMAGE

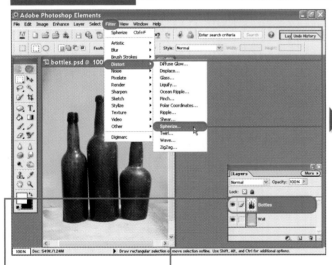

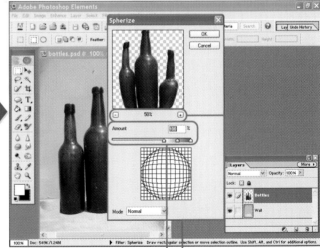

1 Select the layer to which you want to apply the filter.

Note: For more about layers, see Chapter 9.

2 Click **Filter**.

3 Click **Distort**.

4 Click **Spherize**.

■ The Spherize dialog box appears.

■ A small window displays a preview of the filter's effect.

5 Click 🔳 or ➕ to zoom out or in.

6 Click and drag the Amount slider (△) to control the amount of distortion added.

What happens when I type a negative value in the Amount field of the Spherize dialog box?

A negative value "squeezes" the shapes in your image instead of expanding them. The Pinch filter — which you can also find under the **Filter** and **Distort** menu selections — produces a similar effect.

■ In this example, the intensity of the spherize effect has been decreased.

7 Click **OK**.

■ Elements applies the filter.

ADD NOISE TO AN IMAGE

Filters in the Noise menu add or remove graininess in your image. You can add graininess with the Add Noise filter.

To apply the filter to just part of your image, you can make a selection with a selection tool. To use the selection tools, see Chapter 4.

ADD NOISE TO AN IMAGE

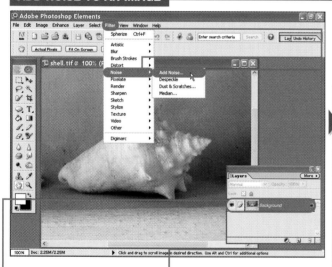

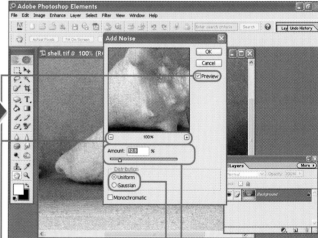

1 Select the layer to which you want to apply the filter.

Note: For more about layers, see Chapter 9.

■ In this example, the image has a single background layer.

2 Click **Filter**.

3 Click **Noise**.

4 Click **Add Noise**.

■ The Add Noise dialog box appears displaying a preview.

5 Click ⊟ or ⊞ to zoom out or in.

6 Click **Preview** to preview the effect in the main window (☐ changes to ☑).

7 Click and drag the Amount slider (⌂) to change the noise.

8 Click here to select how you want the noise distributed (○ changes to ◉).

■ Uniform spreads the noise more evenly than Gaussian.

What does the Monochromatic setting in the Add Noise dialog box do?

If you click **Monochromatic** (☐ changes to ☑), Elements adds noise by lightening or darkening pixels in your image. Pixel hues stay the same. At high settings with the Monochromatic setting on, the filter produces a television-static effect.

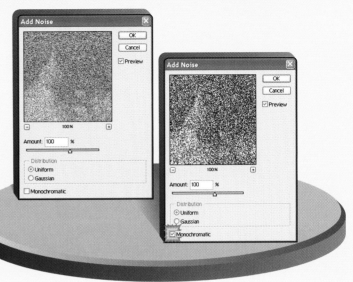

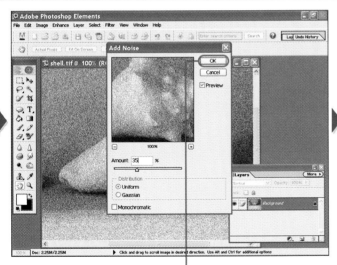

■ In this example, the Amount value has been increased.

9 Click **OK**.

■ Elements applies the filter.

TURN AN IMAGE INTO SHAPES

The Pixelate filters divide areas of your image into solid-colored dots or shapes. The Crystallize filter, one example of a Pixelate filter, re-creates your image using colored polygons.

To apply the filter to just part of your image, you can make a selection with a selection tool. To use the selection tools, see Chapter 4.

TURN AN IMAGE INTO SHAPES

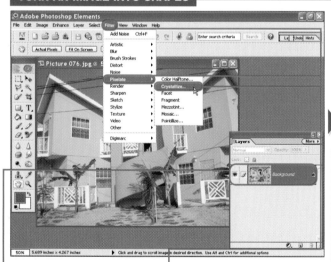

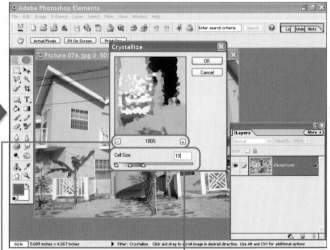

1 Select the layer to which you want to apply the filter.

Note: For more about layers, see Chapter 9.

■ In this example, the image has a single background layer.

2 Click **Filter**.

3 Click **Pixelate**.

4 Click **Crystallize**.

■ The Crystallize dialog appears displaying a preview of the filter's effect.

5 Click ⊟ or ⊞ to zoom out or in.

6 Click and drag the Cell Size slider (⌂) to adjust the size of the shapes.

■ The size can range from 3 to 300.

What does the Mosaic filter do?

The Mosaic filter converts your image to a set of solid-color squares. You can control the size of the squares in the filter's dialog box. To apply the filter:

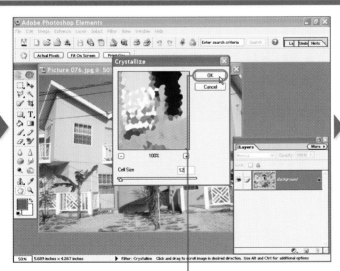

1 Click **Filter**.

2 Click **Pixelate**.

3 Click **Mosaic**.

■ The Mosaic dialog box opens.

4 Click and drag △ to specify the mosaic square size.

5 Click **OK**.

■ Elements applies the filter.

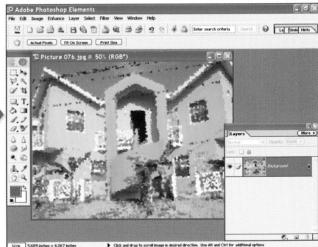

■ In this example, the Cell Size has been slightly increased.

7 Click **OK**.

■ Elements applies the filter.

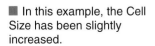

TURN AN IMAGE INTO A CHARCOAL SKETCH

The Sketch filters add outlining effects to your image. The Charcoal filter, for example, makes an image look as if you sketched it using charcoal on paper.

Elements uses the foreground as the charcoal color and the background as the paper color. Changing these changes the filter's effect. See Chapter 7 to adjust color.

To apply the filter to just part of your image, you can make the selection with a selection tool. To use the selection tools, see Chapter 4.

TURN AN IMAGE INTO A CHARCOAL SKETCH

1 Select the layer to which you want to apply the filter.

Note: For more about layers, see Chapter 9.

■ In this example, the image has a single background layer.

2 Click **Filter**.

3 Click **Sketch**.

4 Click **Charcoal**.

■ The Charcoal dialog box appears.

■ A small window displays a preview of the filter's effect.

5 Click 🔽 or 🔼 to zoom out or in.

6 Click and drag the sliders (△) to control the filter's effect.

What does the Photocopy filter do?

The Photocopy filter converts your image's shadows and midtones to the foreground color and highlights to the background color. The result is an image that looks photocopied. To apply the filter:

1 Click **Filter**.

2 Click **Sketch**.

3 Click **Photocopy**.

■ The Photocopy dialog box opens.

4 Click and drag △ to control the detail and darkness of the colors.

5 Click **OK**.

■ Elements applies the filter.

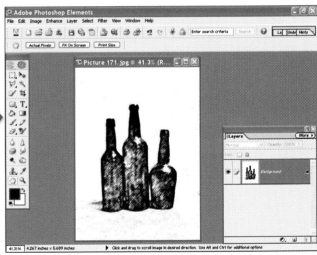

■ In this example, the thickness of the charcoal strokes has been increased. The Light/Dark Balance setting has also been increased to darken the image.

7 Click **OK**.

■ Elements applies the filter.

APPLY GLOWING EDGES TO AN IMAGE

The Glowing Edges filter, one example of a Stylize filter, applies a neon effect to the edges in your image. Areas between the edges turn black. Other Stylize filters produce similarly extreme artistic effects.

To apply the filter to just part of your image, you can make a selection with a selection tool. To use the selection tools, see Chapter 4.

APPLY GLOWING EDGES TO AN IMAGE

1 Select the layer to which you want to apply the filter.

Note: For more about layers, see Chapter 9.

■ In this example, the image has a single background layer.

2 Click **Filter**.

3 Click **Stylize**.

4 Click **Glowing Edges**.

■ The Glowing Edges dialog box appears.

■ A small window displays a preview of the filter's effect.

5 Click 🗆 or 🞧 to zoom out or in.

6 Click and drag the sliders (△) to control intensity of the glow you add to the edges in the image.

What is the Find Edges filter?

The Find Edges filter is similar to the Glowing Edges filter except that it places white pixels between the edges in your image. Find Edges is a one-step filter, which means you cannot fine-tune its effects in a dialog box before you apply it. To apply the filter:

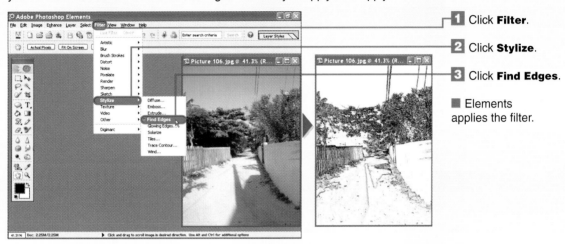

1 Click **Filter**.

2 Click **Stylize**.

3 Click **Find Edges**.

■ Elements applies the filter.

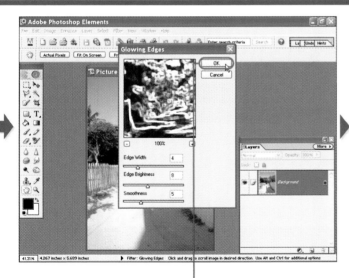

■ In this example, the Edge Width and Edge Brightness values have been increased to intensify the neon effect.

7 Click **OK**.

■ Elements applies the filter.

ADD TEXTURE TO AN IMAGE

You can overlay different textures on your image with the Texturizer filter. The other Texture filters let you apply other patterns.

To apply the filter to just part of your image, you can make a selection with a selection tool. See Chapter 4 to use the selection tools.

ADD TEXTURE TO AN IMAGE

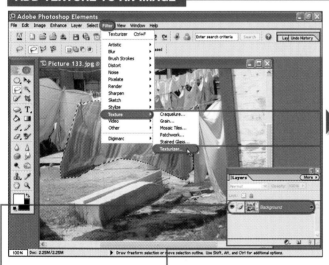

1 Select the layer to which you want to apply the filter.

Note: For more about layers, see Chapter 9.

■ In this example, a selection has been made in the single background layer.

2 Click **Filter**.

3 Click **Texture**.

4 Click **Texturizer**.

■ The Texturizer dialog box appears.

■ A small window displays a preview of the filter's effect.

5 Click 🔲 or 🔲 to zoom out or in.

6 Click ✓ (🔲).

7 Select a texture to apply.

What does the Stained Glass filter do?

The Stained Glass filter converts small areas of your image into different solid-color shapes, similar to those you might see in a stained-glass window. A foreground-color border separates the shapes. To apply the filter:

1 Click **Filter**.

2 Click **Texture**.

3 Click **Stained Glass**.

■ The Stained Glass dialog box opens.

4 Click and drag △ to control the size and shape of the cells.

5 Click **OK**.

■ Elements applies the filter.

8 Click and drag the sliders (△) to control the scale and intensity of the overlaid texture.

9 Click ⌄ (⬆) and click a light direction.

10 Click **OK**.

■ Elements applies the filter.

CAST A SPOTLIGHT ON AN IMAGE

The Lighting Effects filter lets you add spotlight and other lighting enhancements to your image. You may find it useful for highlighting an object in your photographic art.

To apply the filter to just part of your image, you can make a selection with a selection tool. To use the selection tools, see Chapter 4.

CAST A SPOTLIGHT ON AN IMAGE

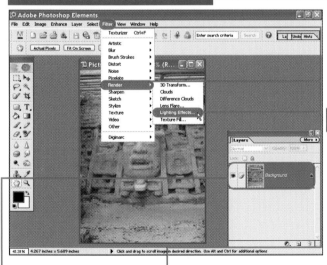

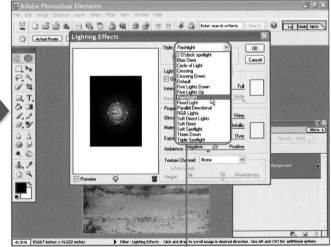

1 Select the layer to which you want to apply the filter.

Note: For more about layers, see Chapter 9.

■ In this example, the image has a single background layer.

2 Click **Filter**.

3 Click **Render**.

4 Click **Lighting Effects**.

■ The Lighting Effects dialog box appears.

■ Elements displays a small preview of the effect.

5 Click ⌄ (⬧) and click a lighting style.

What is a lens flare, and how can I add it to an image?

Lens flare is the extra flash of light that sometimes appears in a photo when too much light enters a camera lens. Although photographers try to avoid this effect, you can add it to make your digital image look more like an old-fashioned photograph. To apply the filter:

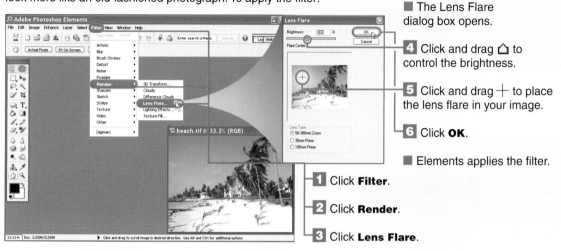

■ The Lens Flare dialog box opens.

4 Click and drag △ to control the brightness.

5 Click and drag ✛ to place the lens flare in your image.

6 Click **OK**.

■ Elements applies the filter.

1 Click **Filter**.

2 Click **Render**.

3 Click **Lens Flare**.

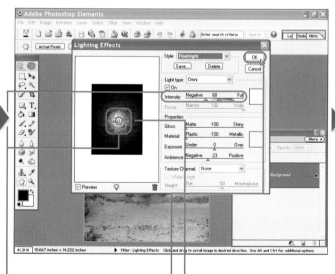

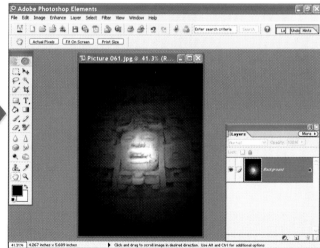

6 Click and drag the Intensity slider ( ) to control the light intensity.

7 Adjust the position and shape of the lighting by clicking and dragging the handles in the preview window.

■ You can click and drag the center point to change where the light is centered.

8 Click **OK**.

■ Elements applies the filter.

EMBOSS AN IMAGE

You can achieve the effect of a three-dimensional shape pressed into paper with the Emboss filter. You may find this filter useful for generating textured backgrounds.

To apply the filter to just part of your image, you can make a selection with a selection tool. To use the selection tools, see Chapter 4.

EMBOSS AN IMAGE

1 Select the layer to which you want to apply the filter.

Note: For more about layers, see Chapter 9.

■ In this example, the image has a single background layer.

2 Click **Filter**.

3 Click **Stylize**.

4 Click **Emboss**.

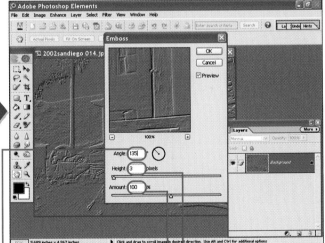

■ The Emboss dialog box appears.

■ Elements displays a small preview of the effect.

5 Type an angle to specify in which direction to shadow the image.

6 Type a height from 1 to 10 to specify the strength of the embossing.

7 Type an amount from 1 to 500 to specify the number of edges the filter affects.

Do I have another way to create an embossed effect in an image?

Yes. You can use the Bas Relief filter to get a similar effect. It creates a two-toned embossed effect by reducing an image to the current foreground and background colors. To apply the filter:

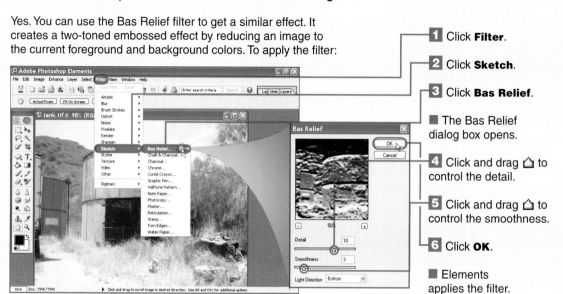

1 Click **Filter**.

2 Click **Sketch**.

3 Click **Bas Relief**.

■ The Bas Relief dialog box opens.

4 Click and drag △ to control the detail.

5 Click and drag △ to control the smoothness.

6 Click **OK**.

■ Elements applies the filter.

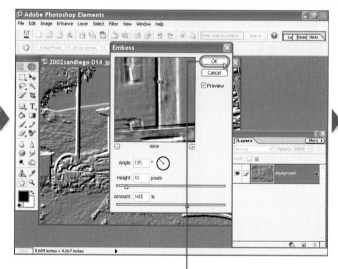

■ In this example, increasing the height and amount magnifies the Emboss effect.

8 Click **OK**.

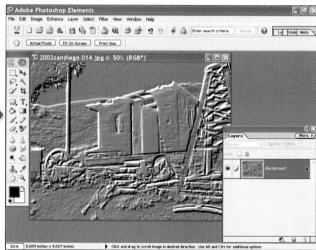

■ Elements applies the filter.

CREATE A CUTOUT IMAGE

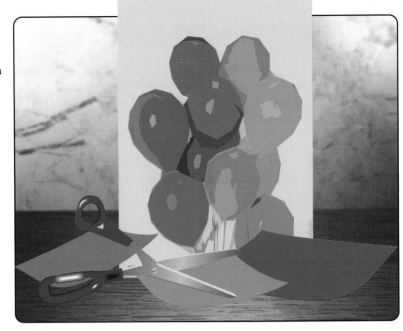

You can convert a detailed photograph into a relatively small number of solid-color blocks with the Cutout filter. The resulting image looks like it is made of construction-paper cutouts.

To apply the filter to just part of your image, you can make a selection with a selection tool. See Chapter 4 to use the selection tools.

CREATE A CUTOUT IMAGE

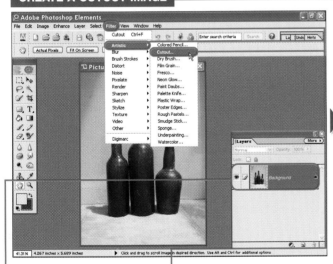

1 Select the layer to which you want to apply the filter.

Note: For more about layers, see Chapter 9.

■ In this example, the image has a single background layer.

2 Click **Filter**.

3 Click **Artistic**.

4 Click **Cutout**.

■ The Cutout dialog box appears.

■ Elements displays a small preview of the effect.

5 Click and drag the No. of Levels △ to specify the number of colors in the resulting image.

6 Click and drag the Edge Simplicity △ to specify the number of edges you want.

7 Click and drag the Edge Fidelity △ to specify how well the solid color edges match the original edges.

How can I easily select the solid colors in an image that has the Cutout filter applied?

You can select the colors by using the Magic Wand tool (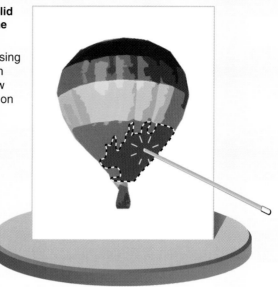) with the tool's tolerance set to a low amount. For more information on using this feature, see p. 64.

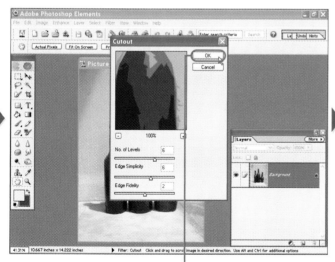

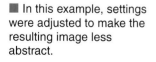

■ In this example, settings were adjusted to make the resulting image less abstract.

8 Click **OK**.

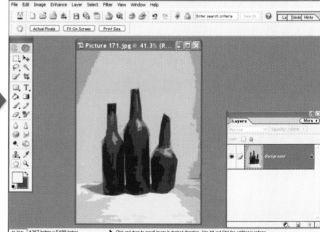

■ Elements applies the filter.

OFFSET AN IMAGE

The filters in the Other submenu produce interesting effects that do not fall under the other menu descriptions. For example, you can shift your image horizontally or vertically in the image window using the Other menu's Offset filter.

To apply the filter to just a specific part of your image, you can make a selection with a selection tool. See Chapter 4 to use the selection tools.

OFFSET AN IMAGE

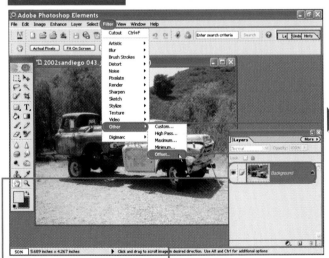

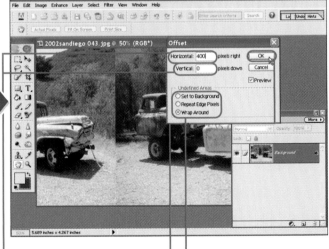

1 Select the layer to which you want to apply the filter.

Note: For more about layers, see Chapter 9.

■ In this example, the image has a single background layer.

2 Click **Filter**.

3 Click **Other**.

4 Click **Offset**.

■ The Offset dialog box appears.

5 Type a horizontal offset.

6 Type a vertical offset.

7 Click an option to select how you want Elements to treat pixels at the edge (○ changes to ⦿).

8 Click **OK**.

How do I make a seamless tile?

Seamless tiles are images that when laid side by side leave no noticeable seam where they meet. You often use them as background images for Web pages. To create a seamless tile, start with an evenly textured image; offset the image horizontally and vertically; then clean up the resulting seams with the Clone Stamp tool ( ). See Chapter 8 for information on using this feature. The resulting image tiles seamlessly when you use it as a Web page background.

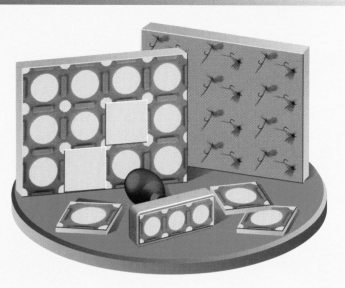

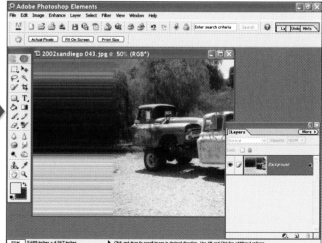

■ In this example, the image has been shifted horizontally (to the right) by adding a positive value to the horizontal field.

■ Wrap Around option was selected, so the pixels that leave the right edge of the image reappear on the left edge.

■ In this example, the same offset was applied but with the Repeat Edge Pixels selected. This creates a streaked effect at the left edge.

USING THE LIQUIFY TOOLS

Elements' Liquify tools enable you to dramatically warp areas of your image. The tools are useful for making your image look like it is melting.

To apply the filter to just a select part of your image, you can make a selection with a selection tool. See Chapter 4 to use the selection tools.

USING THE LIQUIFY TOOL

1 Select the layer to which you want to apply the Liquify tool.

Note: For more about layers, see Chapter 9.

■ In this example, the image has a single background layer.

2 Click **Filter**.

3 Click **Distort**.

4 Click **Liquify**.

■ The Liquify dialog box displays.

5 Click a Liquify tool.

6 Type a Brush Size from 1 to 150.

7 Type a Brush Pressure (strength) from 1 to 100.

What do the different Liquify tools do?

The Warp tool (🖐) pushes pixels in the direction you drag.

The Turbulence tool (≋) applies waves as you drag it.

The Twirl Clockwise tool (⟳) produces a clockwise whirlpool effect.

The Twirl Counterclockwise tool (⟲) produces a counterclockwise whirlpool effect.

The Pucker tool (🔲) pushes pixels toward the brush center.

The Bloat tool (🔲) pushes pixels away from the brush center.

The Shift Pixels tool (🔲) pushes pixels perpendicular to the direction you drag.

The Reflection tool (🔲) reflects pixels as you drag.

The Reconstruct tool (🖌) restores pixels to their original state.

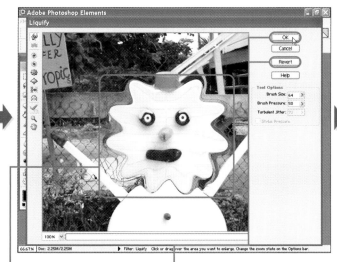

■8 Click and drag inside the image window.

■ Elements liquifies the image where you drag the brush.

■ You can click **Revert** to change the image back to its original state.

■9 Click **OK**.

■ Elements applies the Liquify effect to your image.

CHAPTER 12

Adding and Manipulating Type

Do you want to add letters and words to your photos and illustrations? Photoshop Elements lets you add type to your images and precisely control the type's appearance and layout. You can also stylize your type using Elements' filters and other tools.

ADD HORIZONTAL TYPE TO AN IMAGE

Adding type enables you to label elements in your image or use letters and words in artistic ways. You may find horizontal type useful for titles and captions.

ADD HORIZONTAL TYPE TO AN IMAGE

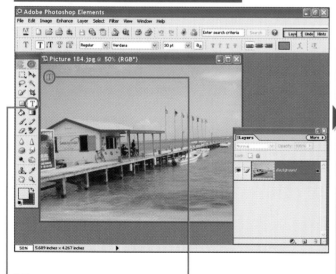

1 Click the Type tool (T).

2 Click where you want the new type to begin.

3 Click ⌄ and select a style, font, and size for your type.

4 Click the Color box (■) to select a color for your type.

Note: Elements applies the foreground color by default. See Chapter 6 for more about selecting colors.

How do I reposition my type?

You can move the layer that contains the type with the Move tool (). Click the layer of type, click , and then click and drag to reposition your type. For more on moving a layer, see Chapter 9.

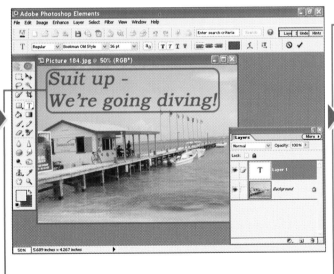

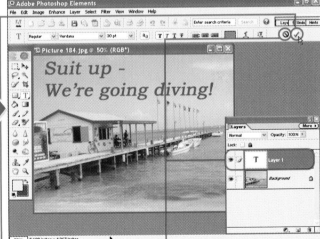

5 Type your text.

■ To create a line break, press **Enter** (**Return**).

6 When you finish typing your text, click ✓ or press **Enter** on your keyboard's number pad.

■ You can click ⊘ or press **Esc** (⌘ + .) to cancel.

■ Elements places the type in its own layer.

ADD VERTICAL TYPE TO AN IMAGE

You can create vertical type to make interesting labels or signs in your images. A button on the Options bar lets you switch vertical type to horizontal type, and back again.

ADD VERTICAL TYPE TO AN IMAGE

ADD VERTICAL TYPE

1 Click and hold T.

2 Click the Vertical Type Tool button (T) in the menu that appears.

3 Click where you want the new type to appear.

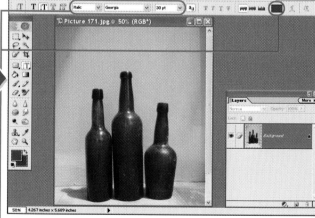

4 Click ⌄ and select a style, font, and size for your type.

5 Click the Color box (▮) to select a color for your type.

Note: Elements applies the foreground color by default. See Chapter 6 for more about selecting colors.

How do I rotate type?

You can rotate type in your image by
rotating the layer that contains the type:

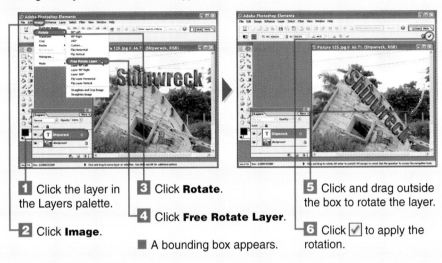

1 Click the layer in
the Layers palette.

2 Click **Image**.

3 Click **Rotate**.

4 Click **Free Rotate Layer**.

■ A bounding box appears.

5 Click and drag outside
the box to rotate the layer.

6 Click ☑ to apply the
rotation.

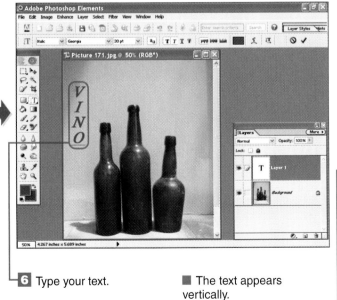

6 Type your text.

■ The text appears
vertically.

**SWITCH THE TYPE
TO HORIZONTAL**

1 Click the layer containing
the vertical type you want to
switch.

2 Click the Change the Text
Orientation button (⊥).

■ Elements switches the
vertical text to horizontal.

EDIT TYPE

You can edit type to change letters, words, or sentences.

EDIT TYPE

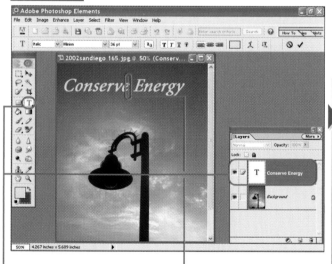

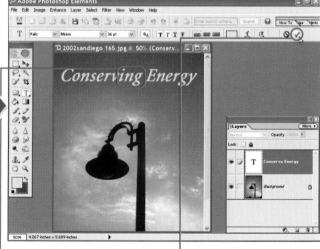

1 Click T.

2 Click the type layer that you want to edit.

Note: If the Layers palette is not visible, see Chapter 1 to open it.

3 Click inside the type at the place that you want to edit.

■ A blinking cursor (|) appears.

4 Press **+Backspace** or **Delete** to delete characters.

5 Type to add new characters.

■ You can use arrow keys (↑, ↓, →, ←) to move within your type.

6 When you finish typing your text, click ✓ or press **Enter** on your keyboard's number pad.

■ Element applies your changes.

You can delete a type
layer to remove its type
from your image.

DELETE TYPE

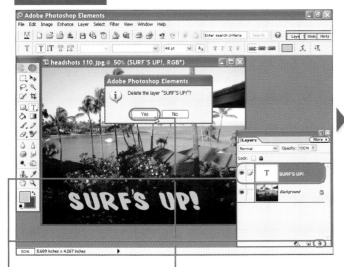

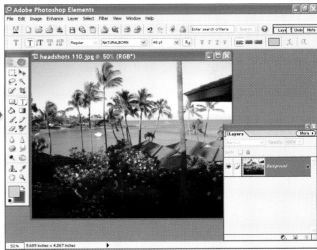

■1 Click the type layer that
you want to delete.

■2 Click 🗑.

■ A dialog box appears
asking if you want to delete
the layer.

■3 Click **Yes**.

■ Elements deletes the
layer and the type inside it.

CHANGE THE FORMATTING OF TYPE

You can change the font, style, size, and other characteristics of your type.

CHANGE THE FORMATTING OF TYPE

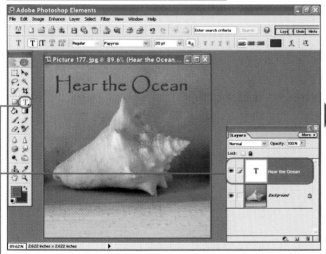

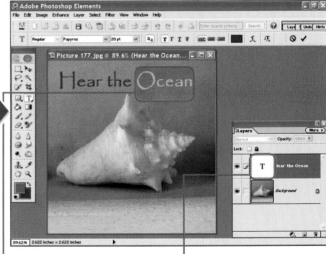

■1 Click T.

■2 Click the type layer that you want to edit.

Note: If the Layers palette is not visible, see Chapter 1 to open it.

■3 Click and drag to select some type from the selected layer.

■ You can double-click the layer thumbnail to select all the type.

What is antialiasing?

Antialiasing is the process of adding semitransparent pixels to curved edges in digital images to make the edges appear smoother. You can apply antialiasing to type to improve its appearance. Text that you do not antialias can sometimes look jagged. You can control the presence and style of your type's antialiasing with the Options bar.

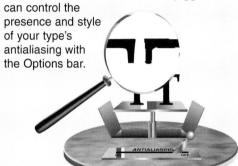

How do I change the alignment of my type?

When creating your text, click one of the three alignment buttons: Left align text (⬛), Center text (⬛), or Right align text (⬛). You may find these options useful when you create multiline passages of type.

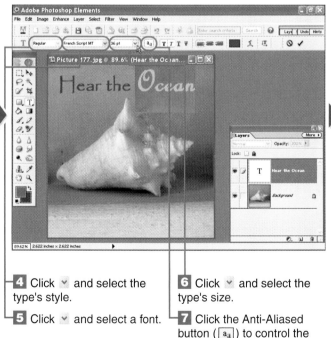

4 Click ⌄ and select the type's style.

5 Click ⌄ and select a font.

6 Click ⌄ and select the type's size.

7 Click the Anti-Aliased button (a꜀) to control the type's antialiasing.

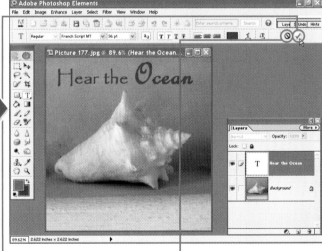

8 When you finish formatting your text, click ✓ or press **Enter** on your keyboard's number pad.

■ You can click ⊘ or press **Esc** (⌘+.) to cancel.

■ Elements applies the formatting to your type.

CHANGE THE COLOR OF TYPE

You can change the color
of your type to make it
blend or contrast with
the rest of the image.

CHANGE THE COLOR OF TYPE

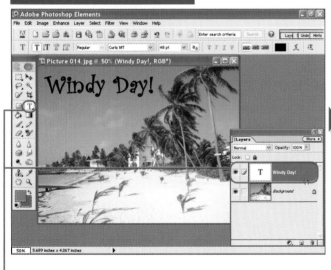

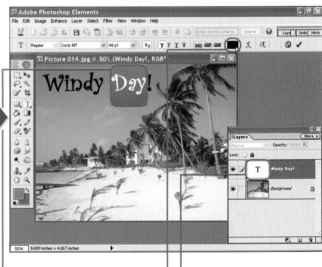

1 Click T.

2 Click the type layer that
you want to edit.

*Note: If the Layers palette is not
visible, see Chapter 1 to open it.*

3 Click and drag to select
some text.

■ You can double-click the
layer thumbnail to select all
the type.

4 Click ■.

How do I change type color using the Swatches palette?

The Swatches palette offers an alternative to the
Color Picker dialog box when choosing colors:

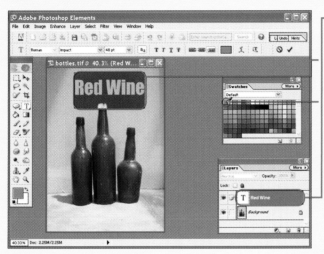

1 Click the type layer
in the Layers palette.

2 Click and drag in the image window
to select the text you want to recolor.

3 Click a color in the
Swatches palette.

*Note: See Chapter 1 to learn how to open
the Layers and the Swatches palettes.*

■ The type changes color.

■ To see the actual new color, click
away from the type in the image
window to deselect it.

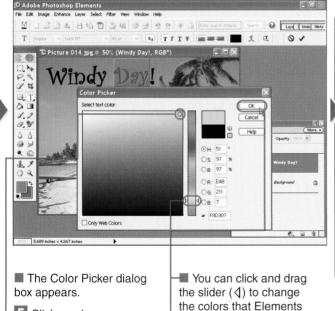

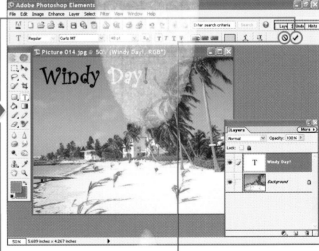

■ The Color Picker dialog
box appears.

5 Click a color.

■ You can click and drag
the slider (◁) to change
the colors that Elements
displays in the window.

6 Click **OK**.

7 Click ✓ or press `Enter`
on your keyboard's number
pad.

■ You can click ⊘ or press
`Esc` (⌘ + .) to cancel.

■ Elements changes the
text to the new color.

APPLY A FILTER TO TYPE

You can add interesting effects to your type with Elements' filters. To apply a filter to type, you must first simplify it. *Simplifying* converts your type layer into a regular Elements layer. You can no longer edit simplified type using the type tools.

APPLY A FILTER TO TYPE

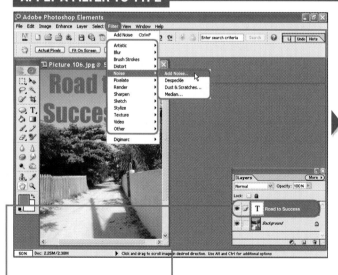

1 Select the type layer to which you want to apply a filter.

Note: If the Layers palette is not visible, see Chapter 1 to open it.

2 Click **Filter**.

3 Click a filter submenu.

4 Click a filter.

■ A dialog box appears asking if you want to simplify the layer.

5 Click **OK**.

How can I create semitransparent type?

Select the type layer in the Layers palette and then reduce the layer's opacity to less than 100%. This makes the type semitransparent. For details about changing opacity, see p. 166.

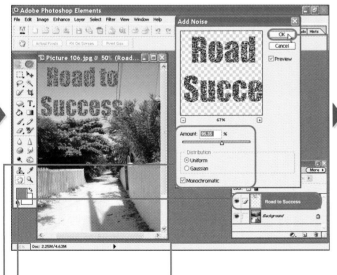

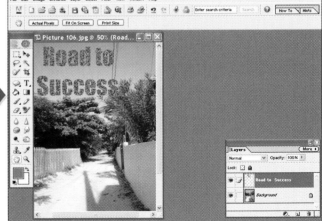

■ Elements converts the type layer to a regular layer.

6 Specify your filter settings.

Note: For more information on filter settings, see Chapter 11.

7 Click **OK**.

■ Elements applies the filter to the text.

■ In this example, noise was added to the type with the Add Noise filter.

WARP TYPE

Elements' Warp feature lets you easily bend and distort layers of type. This can help you stylize your type to match the theme of your image.

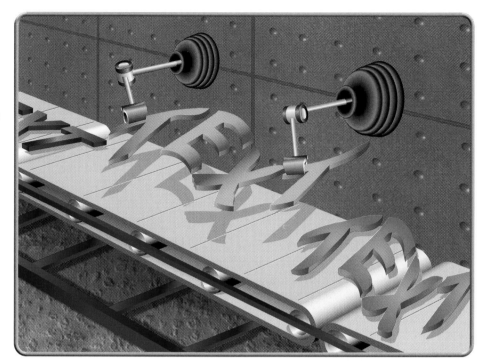

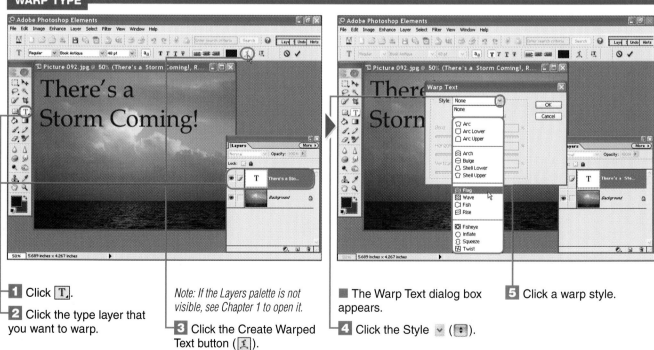

1 Click T.

2 Click the type layer that you want to warp.

Note: If the Layers palette is not visible, see Chapter 1 to open it.

3 Click the Create Warped Text button (工).

■ The Warp Text dialog box appears.

4 Click the Style ∨ (⬦).

5 Click a warp style.

246

How do I unwarp type?

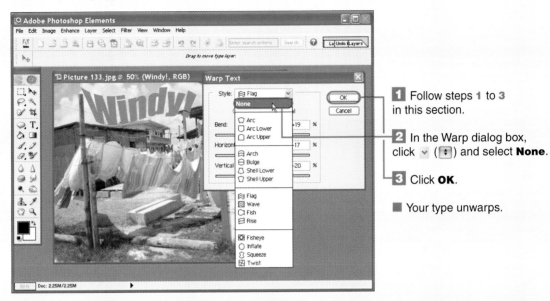

1 Follow steps **1** to **3** in this section.

2 In the Warp dialog box, click ∨ (⬍) and select **None**.

3 Click **OK**.

■ Your type unwarps.

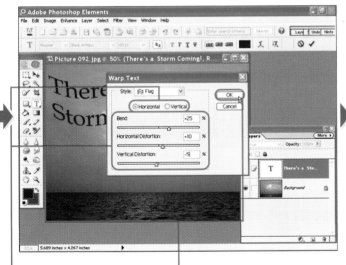

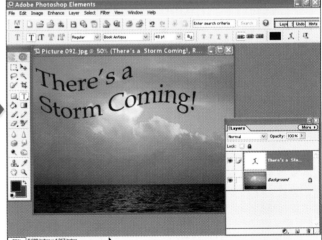

6 Click an orientation for the warp effect (○ changes to ◉).

7 Adjust the Bend and Distortion values by clicking and dragging the sliders (△).

■ The Bend and Distortion values determine the intensity of the warp.

■ For all settings, a value of 0% means Elements does not apply a warp.

8 Click **OK**.

■ Elements warps the text.

■ You can still edit the format, color, and other characteristics of the type when you apply warp.

OUTLINE TYPE

You can create outlined type to make letters and words in your images stand out.

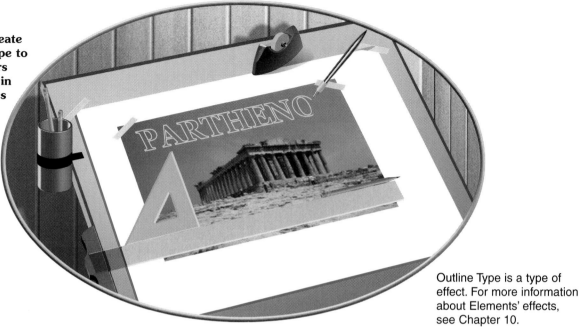

Outline Type is a type of effect. For more information about Elements' effects, see Chapter 10.

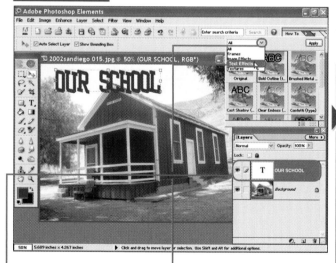

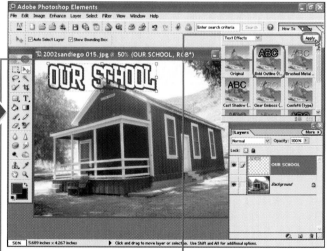

1 Click the type layer that you want to outline.

2 Open the Effects palette.

Note: If the Effects palette is not visible, see Chapter 1 to open it.

3 Click ☑ (⬍).

4 Click **Text Effects**.

5 Click an outline effect — **Thin Outline**, **Medium Outline**, or **Bold Outline**.

6 Click **Apply**.

■ Elements applies the effect to the text.

You can cast a shadow
next to your type to give
the type a 3-D look.

Cast a Shadow is a type of
effect. For more information
about Elements' effects, see
Chapter 10.

CAST A SHADOW WITH TYPE

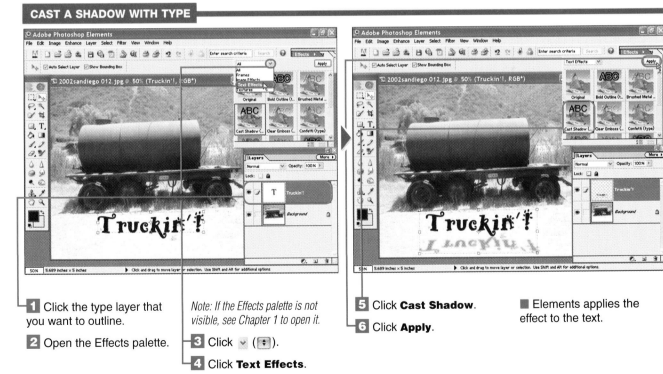

1 Click the type layer that
you want to outline.

2 Open the Effects palette.

*Note: If the Effects palette is not
visible, see Chapter 1 to open it.*

3 Click ⌄ (⬍).

4 Click **Text Effects**.

5 Click **Cast Shadow**.

6 Click **Apply**.

■ Elements applies the
effect to the text.

CHAPTER 13

Automating Your Work

Sometimes you want to perform the same simple sequence of commands on a lot of different images. With Elements' batch commands, you can automatically convert the file type or change the size of every image file in a folder. Other Elements features make it easy to automatically create Web photo galleries, picture packages, and panoramic images.

CONVERT FILE TYPES

You can convert all the image files in a folder to a specific file type. You may find this useful if you want to post a number of pictures on the Web and need the images in a Web file format such as GIF or JPEG.

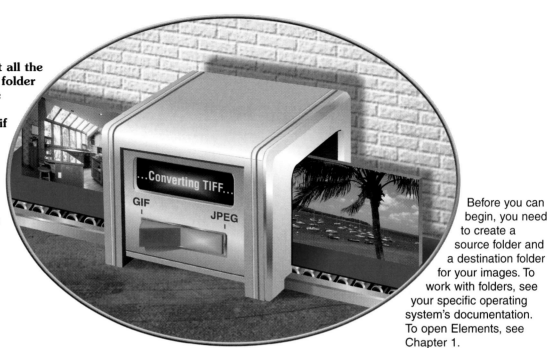

Before you can begin, you need to create a source folder and a destination folder for your images. To work with folders, see your specific operating system's documentation. To open Elements, see Chapter 1.

CONVERT FILE TYPES

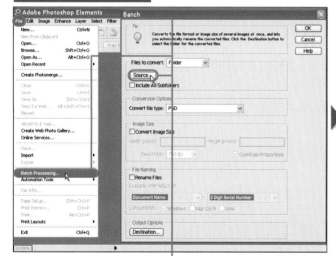

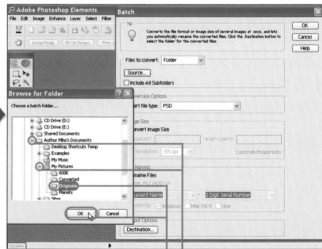

1 Place the images you want to convert into a source folder.

2 Create an empty destination folder in which to save your converted files.

3 In Elements, click **File**.

4 Click **Batch Processing**.

■ The Batch dialog box opens.

5 Click **Source**.

■ In Windows, the Browse for Folders dialog box appears. On a Mac, the Choose a batch folder dialog box appears.

6 In Windows, click ⊞ to open folders. On a Mac, click the folder name to view its contents.

7 Click the folder containing your images.

8 Click **OK (Choose)**.

How do I rename the image files that I convert?

You can rename files using settings in the Batch dialog box:

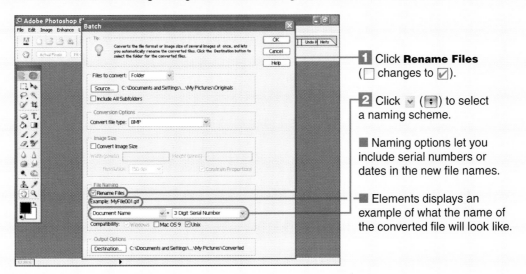

1 Click **Rename Files**
(☐ changes to ☑).

2 Click ☑ (🖸) to select
a naming scheme.

■ Naming options let you
include serial numbers or
dates in the new file names.

■ Elements displays an
example of what the name of
the converted file will look like.

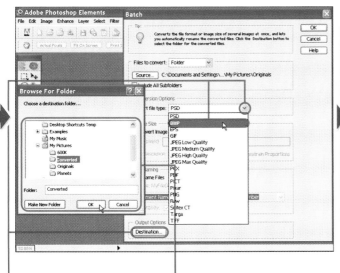

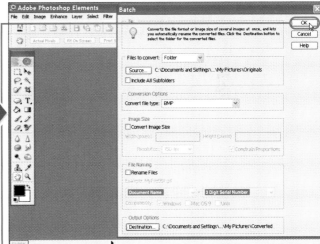

9 Click the Convert file
type ☑ (🖸).

10 Click a file type to which
you want to convert.

11 Click **Destination**.

■ In Windows, the Browse
for Folder dialog box opens.
On a Mac, the Choose a
destination folder dialog
box appears.

12 Repeat steps **6** through
8 to select the folder where
you want the converted files
saved.

13 Click **OK**.

■ Elements cycles through
the image files in the source
folder.

■ Elements converts the
image files and saves the
new versions in the
destination folder.

CONVERT IMAGE SIZES

You can resize all the image files in a folder to specific dimensions. You may find this useful if you want to quickly convert a number of large files from a digital camera to smaller versions that you can store and view more efficiently.

Before you can begin, you need to create a source folder and a destination folder for your images. To work with folders, see your specific operating system's documentation. To open Elements, see Chapter 1.

CONVERT IMAGE SIZES

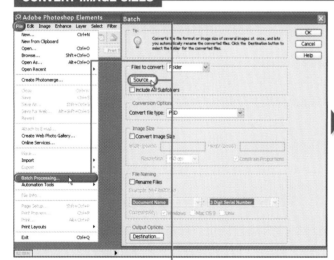

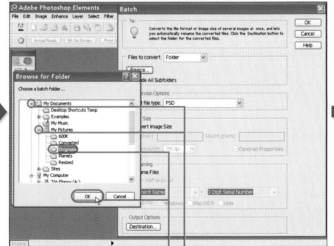

1 Place the images you want to resize into a source folder.

2 Create an empty destination folder in which to save your resized files.

3 In Elements, click **File**.

4 Click **Batch Processing**.

■ The Batch dialog box opens.

5 Click **Source**.

■ In Windows, the Browse for Folder dialog box opens. On a Mac, the Choose batch folder dialog box appears.

6 In Windows, click ⊞ to open folders. On a Mac, click the folder name to view its contents.

7 Click the folder containing your images.

8 Click **OK (Choose)**.

Can I batch-process files that I currently have open in Elements?

Yes. In the Batch dialog box, just click the Files to convert ☑ (🔹) and select **Opened Files**. Elements saves the processed files to the destination folder.

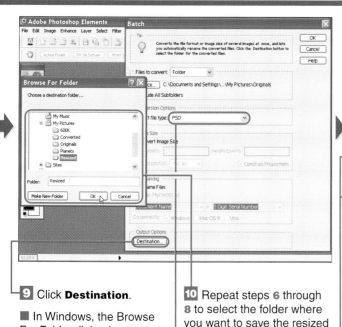

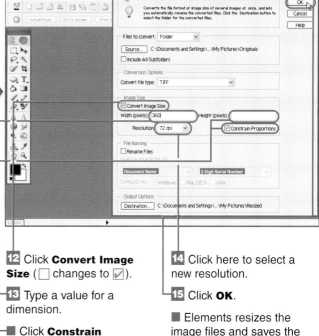

9 Click **Destination**.

■ In Windows, the Browse For Folder dialog box opens. On a Mac, the Choose a destination folder dialog box appears.

10 Repeat steps **6** through **8** to select the folder where you want to save the resized files.

11 Click the Convert file type ☑ (🔹) and select a file type to save the resized files as.

12 Click **Convert Image Size** (☐ changes to ☑).

13 Type a value for a dimension.

■ Click **Constrain Proportions** to size the other dimension automatically.

14 Click here to select a new resolution.

15 Click **OK**.

■ Elements resizes the image files and saves the new versions in the destination folder.

CREATE A CONTACT SHEET

Elements can automatically create a digital version of a photographer's contact sheet. Useful for keeping a hard-copy record of your digital images, contact sheets consist of miniature versions of images that often include identifying and property information.

For information about printing a contact sheet after you have created it, see Chapter 15.

CREATE A CONTACT SHEET

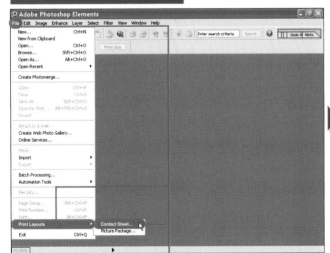

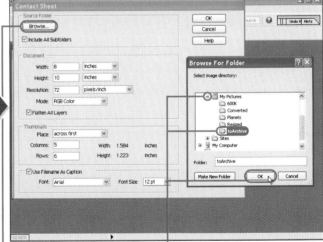

1 Place the images that you want on the contact sheet in a folder.

Note: To work with folders, see your specific operating system's documentation.

2 Click **File**.

3 Click **Print Layouts**.

4 Click **Contact Sheet**.

■ The Contact Sheet dialog box opens.

5 Click **Browse**.

■ In Windows, the Browse For Folder dialog box opens. On a Mac, the Select image directory dialog box opens.

6 In Windows, click ⊞ to open folders. On a Mac, click the folder name to view its contents.

7 Click the folder containing your images.

8 Click **OK (Choose)**.

How do I make the thumbnail images larger on my contact sheet?

Paper size and the number of rows and columns automatically determine the size of the thumbnails. To change the thumbnail size, type a new number of rows and columns in the Columns and Rows boxes in the Contact Sheet dialog box.

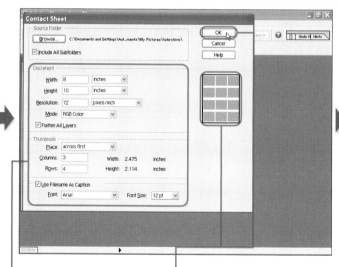

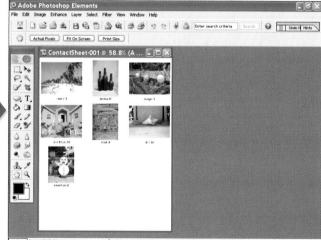

9 Set any contact sheet properties by typing values or by clicking ∨ (↕) and selecting settings.

■ You can set contact sheet size and resolution, the order and number of columns and rows, and the caption font and font size.

■ Elements displays a preview of the layout.

10 Click **OK**.

■ Elements creates and displays your contact sheet.

■ If there are more images than can fit on a single page, Elements creates multiple contact sheets.

CREATE A PICTURE PACKAGE

You can automatically create a one-page layout with a selected image at various sizes using the picture package command. You may find this useful when you want to print out pictures for friends, family, or associates.

For information about printing a picture package after you have created it, see Chapter 15.

CREATE A PICTURE PACKAGE

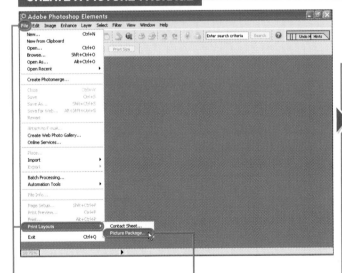

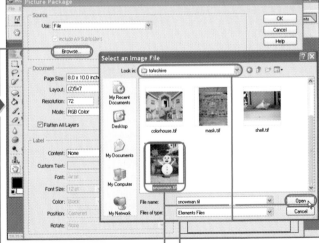

■1 Click **File**.

■2 Click **Print Layouts**.

■3 Click **Picture Package**.

■ The Picture Package dialog box displays.

■4 Click **Browse (Choose)**.

■ In Windows, the Select an Image File dialog box opens. On a Mac, the Please Select a Source File dialog box opens.

■5 In Windows, click ⌄ and select the folder that contains the image file. On a Mac, navigate to find the file you want by scrolling or selecting from the From menu.

■6 Click the image file.

■7 Click **Open**.

How do I add labels to my picture package images?

You can add labels that overlay the picture package images using settings in the Picture Package dialog box:

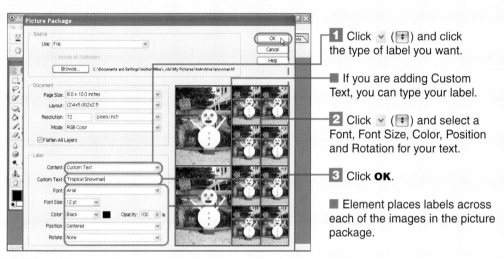

1 Click ⌄ (🔀) and click the type of label you want.

■ If you are adding Custom Text, you can type your label.

2 Click ⌄ (🔀) and select a Font, Font Size, Color, Position and Rotation for your text.

3 Click **OK**.

■ Element places labels across each of the images in the picture package.

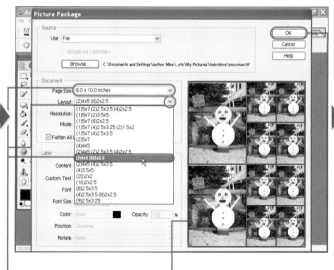

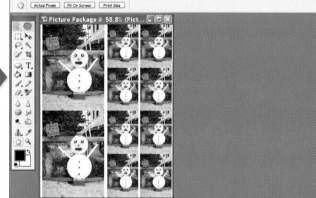

8 Click ⌄ (🔀) and click a page size.

9 Click the Layout ⌄ (🔀).

10 Click a layout.

■ A diagram of the layout appears.

11 Click **OK**.

■ Elements opens a new image window with the picture package image inside it.

CREATE A WEB PHOTO GALLERY

You can have Elements create a photo gallery Web site that showcases your images. Elements not only sizes and optimizes your image files for the site, but it also creates the Web pages that display the images and links those pages together.

After you create your photo gallery, you can use a Web publishing program such as Macromedia Dreamweaver or Adobe GoLive to upload your images to a Web server.

CREATE A WEB PHOTO GALLERY

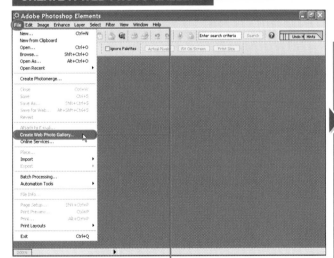

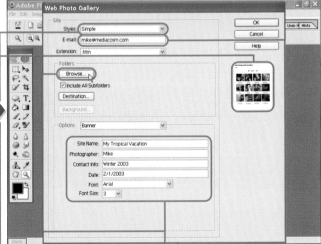

1 Place all the images you want to feature in your Web photo gallery in a folder.

2 Create a separate folder where Elements can save all the image files and HTML files necessary for your gallery.

Note: To work with folders, see your specific operating system's documentation.

3 Click **File**.

4 Click **Create Web Photo Gallery**.

■ The Web Photo Gallery dialog box opens.

5 Click ⌄ (⬦) and click a photo gallery style.

■ Elements displays a preview of the style.

■ You can type an e-mail address to display on the gallery pages.

6 Type values or click ⌄ (⬦) and select the title information for your Web pages.

7 Click **Browse (Choose)**.

How can I customize the pages in my Web photo galleries?

You can customize your pages by selecting different gallery styles. You do this in the Styles menu at the top of the Web Photo Gallery dialog box. The different styles can add themes to your galleries and display the images in different arrangements. You can also select different settings from the Options list to customize image sizes and link colors for the gallery.

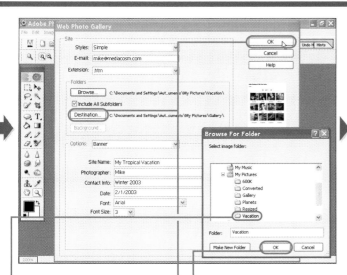

■ In Windows, the Browse For Folder dialog box opens. On a Mac, the Select image directory dialog box opens.

8 Click the folder containing your images.

9 Click **OK (Choose)**.

10 Click **Destination** and repeat steps 8 and 9 to specify the folder in which to save your gallery.

11 Click **OK** in the Web Photo Gallery dialog box.

■ Elements opens each image in the specified folder, creates versions for the photo gallery, and generates the necessary HTML code.

■ After the processing is complete, Elements opens the default Web browser on your computer and displays the home page of the gallery.

■ You can click a thumbnail to see a larger version of the image.

CREATE A PANORAMIC IMAGE

You can use the Photomerge feature in Elements to stitch several images together into a single panoramic image. This allows you to capture more scenery than is usually possible in a regular photograph.

CREATE A PANORAMIC IMAGE

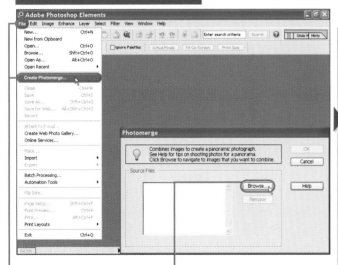

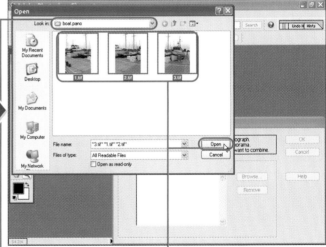

1 Click **File**.

2 Click **Create Photomerge**.

■ The Photomerge dialog box opens.

3 Click **Browse**.

■ The Open dialog box opens.

4 In Windows, click ⌄ , or on a Mac, click ↕ and drag the scroll bar, to select the folder that contains the images that you want to merge.

5 Press **Shift** (⌘) and then click the images you want to merge into a panoramic image.

6 Click **Open**.

How can I create photos that will merge successfully?

To merge photos successfully, you need to align and overlap the photos. Here are a few hints:

• Use a tripod to keep your photos level with one another.

• Refrain from using lenses, such as fisheye lenses, which distort your photos.

• Shoot your photos so that they overlap at least 30%.

For more tips, see the Elements Help documentation.

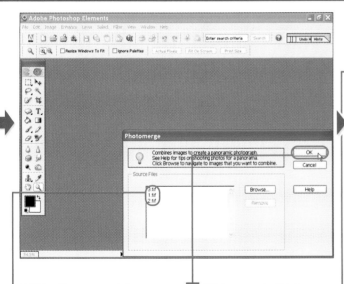

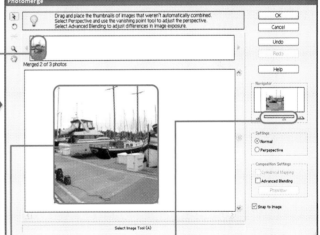

■ The filenames of the images appear in the Source Files list.

7 Click **OK** to build the panoramic image.

■ Elements attempts to merge the images together into a single panoramic image.

■ Thumbnails of the images that it cannot merge appear in a lightbox area.

■ You can click and drag ◢ to zoom the panoramic image in and out.

CONTINUED

CREATE A PANORAMIC IMAGE

The Photomerge dialog box allows you to interactively align the images that make up your panorama.

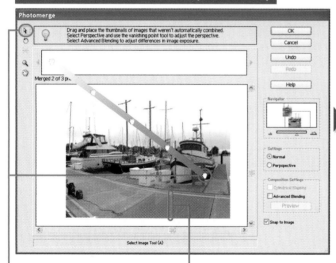

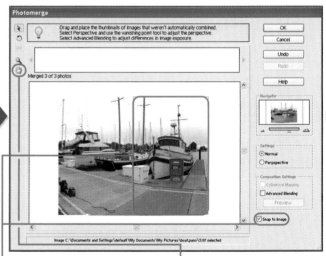

8 Click the Select Image tool ().

9 Click and drag an image from the lightbox to the work area.

10 Place the image so that it lines up with its neighboring image in the panorama.

■ If you select **Snap to Image** (☐ changes to ☑), Elements tries to merge the image edges after you click and drag.

■ You can use the Hand tool () to adjust the placement of the entire panoramic image inside the main window.

11 Repeat steps **8** through **9** for any other images in the lightbox so that they overlap and match one another.

How do I apply perspective to my panorama?

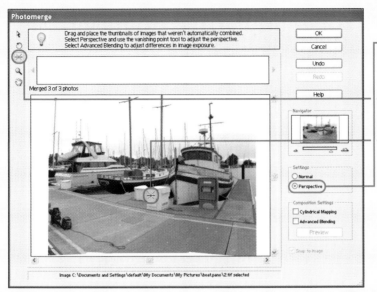

1 In the Photomerge dialog box, click the **Perspective** option (○ changes to ◉).

2 Click the Vanishing Point tool (▦).

3 Click the image to serve as the central focal point for your panorama.

■ When you apply this option, Elements warps the area next to the vanishing point image slightly to provide the correct perspective.

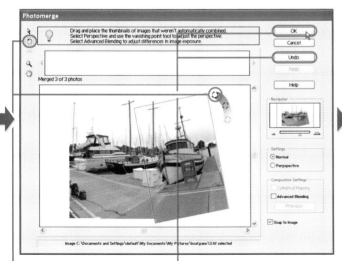

■ You can click the Rotate Image tool (↻) and click and drag with it to align image seams that are not level with one another.

12 Click **OK**.

■ You can click **Undo** to undo your Photomerge commands one at a time.

■ Elements merges the images and opens the new panorama in a new image window.

Note: To save the panorama, see Chapter 14. To print the panorama, see Chapter 15.

E-MAIL AN IMAGE

You can have Elements attach an image to a message in your computer's e-mail program. This allows you to send your imaging projects to other people who are online.

This feature requires you to already have an e-mail program such as Microsoft Outlook, Eudora, or Mac OS X's Mail set up on your computer. Elements does not come with e-mail capability.

E-MAIL AN IMAGE

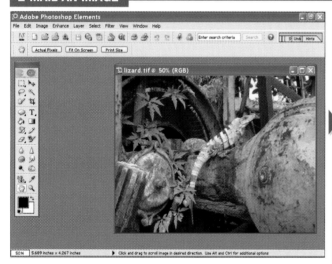

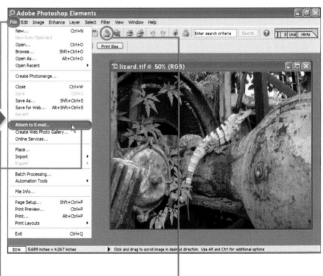

1 Open the image that you want to send via e-mail.

Note: For more about opening images, see Chapter 1.

2 Click **File**.

3 Click **Attach to E-mail**.

■ You can also click 🖼 in the Shortcuts bar.

Why does Elements offer to convert non-JPEG images to JPEG before mailing?

The larger the file size of the mailed image, the longer it takes to receive. The JPEG image format is well suited for creating images that have small file sizes. For example, a TIFF image that is 1 MB in size usually becomes 100K or less as a JPEG. Most e-mail systems also have limits regarding how large an e-mail message can be, which can make using a format such as JPEG a must for your mailed images.

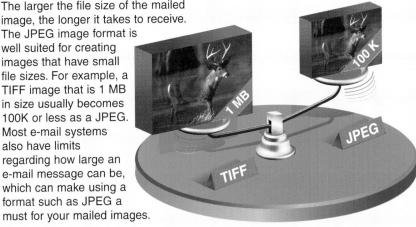

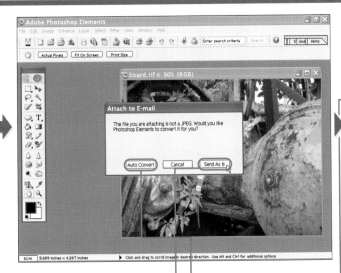

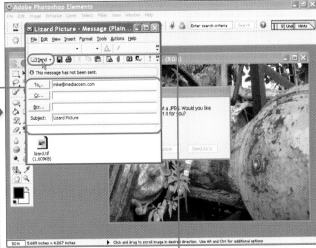

■ If your image is not in the JPEG file format, an Attach to E-mail dialog box appears.

4 You can click **Auto Convert** to automatically save a JPEG copy of your image to send.

■ You can click **Send As Is** to e-mail the image in the non-JPEG format.

■ Elements opens the default e-mail application on your computer and creates a new message with the image attached.

5 Type a recipient e-mail address, a subject line, and other information for the e-mail message.

6 Send the e-mail message.

Note: For more information about using e-mail, see the documentation for the e-mail program on your computer.

CAPTURE AN IMAGE FROM VIDEO

You can open a video clip in Elements and import still frames from it as images. This allows you to edit pictures taken with a video camera just as you would digital camera images or scanned photos.

CAPTURE AN IMAGE FROM VIDEO

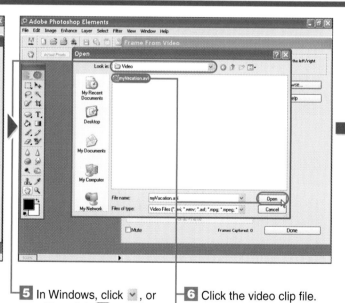

1 Click **File**.

2 Click **Import**.

3 Click **Frame From Video**.

■ The Frame From Video dialog box appears.

4 Click **Browse**.

5 In Windows, click ⌄, or on a Mac click ↕ and drag the scroll bar, to select the folder that contains the video clip file.

6 Click the video clip file.

7 Click **Open**.

How do I get video clips on my computer?

Most digital video cameras let you transfer video clips directly to your computer with a cable. Most non-digital, or *analog*, video cameras require a separate video converter that sits between the computer and camera and converts the analog signal to a digital signal. Make sure that the video clips you save on your computer are in a format that Elements can open. These formats include .avi, .mpg, and .mpeg on PCs, and QuickTime, DV Stream, and .mpeg on Macintosh.

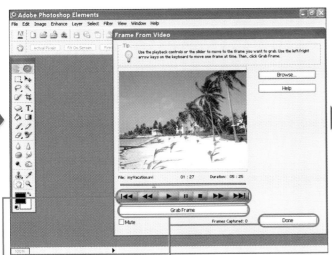

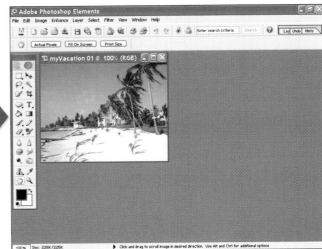

■ **8** Click the control buttons to play the video clip and find a frame to capture:

▶ Play

‖ Pause

◀◀ Rewind

▶▶ Fast Forward

■ You can also click and drag the Scrubber bar (⬦) to find your frame.

■ **9** Click **Grab Frame** to capture a frame.

■ **10** Click **Done**.

■ Elements captures the frame from the video and opens it in a new image window.

■ The size of the new image depends on the video clip frame size.

MAKE A PDF SLIDESHOW

Elements can save several images as a single PDF file that can play as a slideshow. You can set how often the slides change and whether the slideshow repeats.

PDF stands for Portable Document Format, a file format developed by Adobe. You can open PDF files with Adobe Acrobat, which you can download for free at www. adobe.com/acrobat/. Mac OS X's Preview application also opens PDF files.

MAKE A PDF SLIDESHOW

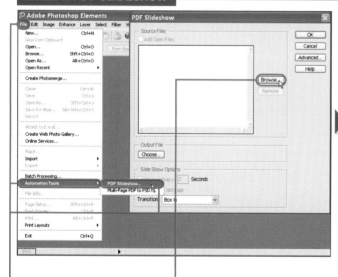

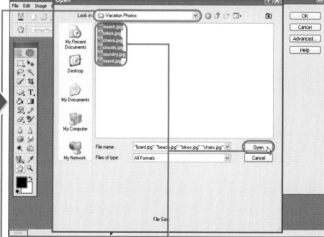

1 Click **File**.

2 Click **Automation Tools**.

3 Click **PDF Slideshow**.

■ The PDF Slideshow dialog box appears.

4 Click **Browse**.

5 In Windows, click ⩒, or on a Mac click ⬍ and drag the scroll bar, to select the folder that contains the images you want to use.

6 Press Shift (⌘) and click to select the images.

7 Click **Open**.

What are slideshow transitions?

Transitions are the effects that occur as one slide in the slideshow replaces another. You can click ⌄ (🔀) and specify one of 18 different transitions in the Transition box located in the PDF Slideshow dialog box. For example, you can make your slides appear in stripes like window blinds with the **Blinds** transitions. With the **Glitter** transitions, new slides appear as randomly scattered squares. **Wipe** transitions bring new slides in from one of the four sides of the screen.

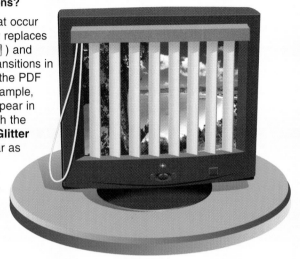

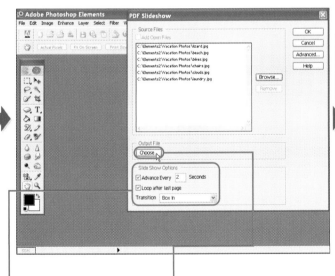

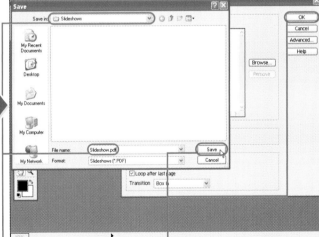

■ Elements lists the files in the Source Files list.

8 Click (☐ changes to ☑) or type values to specify your slideshow options.

■ You can specify how fast the slideshow moves, whether it loops (repeats), and the transition effects that appear between the slides.

9 Click **Choose**.

■ The Save dialog box appears.

10 Click ⌄ (🔀) and select the folder in which to save the slideshow.

11 Type a name for the slideshow.

Note: PDF filenames must end in .pdf.

12 Click **Save**.

13 Click **OK** in the PDF Slideshow dialog box.

■ Elements saves the slideshow.

CHAPTER 14

Saving Files

Do you want to save your files for use later? Or so that you can use them in another application or on the Web? This chapter shows you how.

SAVE IN THE PHOTOSHOP FORMAT

You can save your image in Photoshop's native image format. This format enables you to retain multiple layers in your image, if it has them. This is the best format in which to save your images if you still need to edit them.

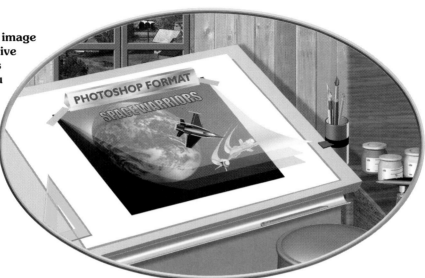

SAVE IN THE PHOTOSHOP FORMAT

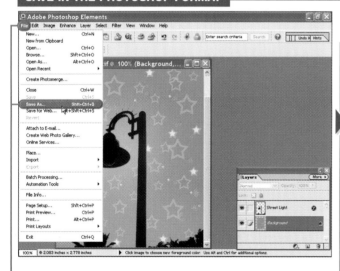

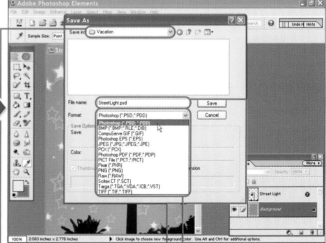

1 Click **File**.

2 Click **Save As**.

■ If you have named and saved your image previously and just want to save changes, you can click **File** and then **Save**.

■ The Save As dialog box appears.

3 In Windows, click ⬇ and then click a folder in which to save the file.

■ On a Mac click ⬍ and then click the column list to locate a folder in which to save the file.

4 Click ⬇ (⬍) and select the Photoshop file format.

5 Type a name for the image file.

274

How do I choose a file format for my image?

You should choose the format based on how you want to use the image. If it is a multilayered image and you want to preserve the layers, save it as a Photoshop file. If you want to use it in word-processing or page-layout applications, save it as a TIFF or EPS file. If you want to use it on the Web, save it as a JPEG, PNG, or GIF file. For more information on file formats, see the rest of this chapter as well as Elements' documentation.

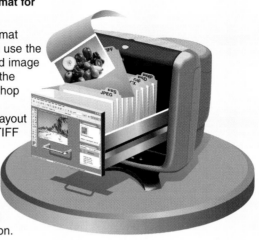

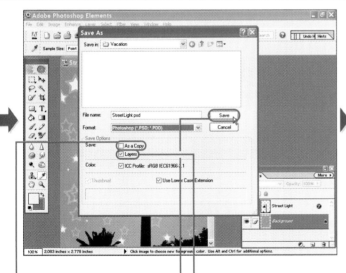

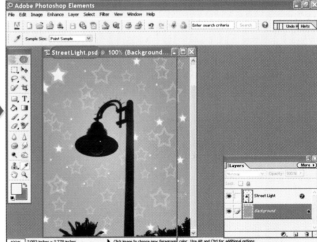

■ Elements automatically assigns a .psd extension.

■ If you want to save a copy of the file and keep the existing file open, click **As a Copy** (☐ changes to ☑).

■ If you want to merge the multiple layers of your image into one layer, click **Layers** (☑ changes to ☐).

6 Click **Save**.

■ Elements saves the image file.

■ The name of the file displays in the image's title bar.

SAVE AN IMAGE FOR USE IN ANOTHER APPLICATION

You can save your image in a format that users can open and use in other imaging or page-layout applications. TIFF, Tagged Image File Format, and EPS, or Encapsulated PostScript, are standard printing formats that many applications on both Windows and Macintosh platforms support.

BMP — bitmap — is a popular Windows image format, and PDF and TIFF are popular Macintosh image formats.

Please note that most image formats — with the exception of the Photoshop, Photoshop PDF, and TIFF formats — do not support layers.

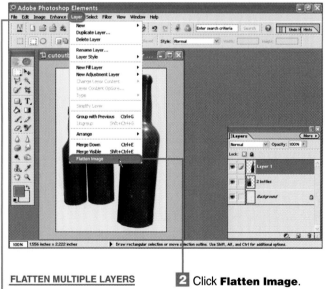

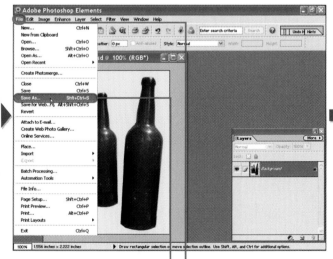

SAVE AN IMAGE FOR USE IN ANOTHER APPLICATION

FLATTEN MULTIPLE LAYERS

1 Click **Layer**.

2 Click **Flatten Image**.

■ If you do not have multiple layers, skip to step **3**.

SAVE THE IMAGE

■ The layers combine into a single layer.

3 Click **File**.

4 Click **Save As**.

■ The Save As dialog box appears.

276

**What are some popular page-
layout programs with which I
might use images?**

Adobe InDesign and
QuarkXPress are two popular
page-layout programs.
They let you combine
text and images to
create brochures,
magazines, and other
printed media. You
can import TIFF and
EPS files saved in
Elements into both
programs.

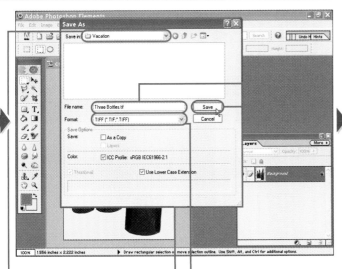

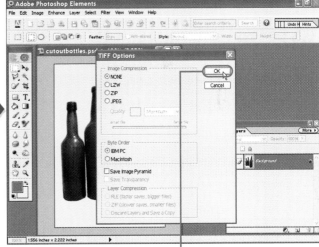

5 In Windows, click ⌄ and
then click a folder in which to
save the file.

■ On a Mac, click ⬍, and
then the column view to
locate a folder in which to
save the file.

6 Click ⌄ (⬍) and select
a file format.

7 Type a filename.

■ Elements automatically
assigns an appropriate
extension for the file format,
such as .tif for TIFF or .eps
for EPS.

8 Click **Save**.

■ In this example, the TIFF
format was selected.

■ A dialog box appears,
enabling you to specify your
file format settings.

9 Click **OK**.

■ Elements saves your
image.

SAVE A JPEG FOR THE WEB

You can save a file in the JPEG — Joint Photographic Experts Group — format and publish it on the Web. JPEG is the preferred file format for saving photographic images.

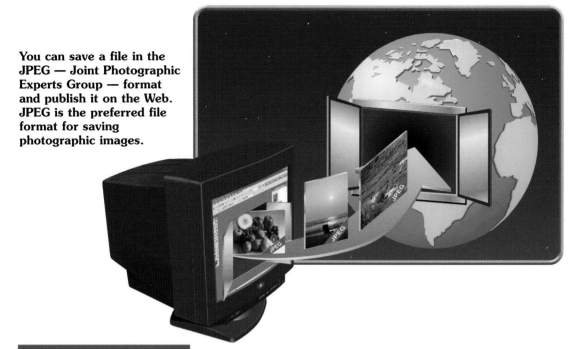

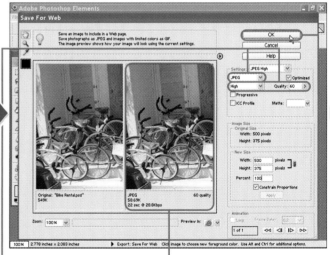

1 Click **File**.

2 Click **Save for Web**.

■ The Save For Web dialog box appears.

3 Click ▾ (⬍) and select **JPEG**.

4 Click here to select a JPEG quality setting.

■ You can select a descriptive setting or a numeric value from 0, low quality, to 100, high quality.

■ The higher the quality, the larger the resulting file.

5 Check that the file quality and size are acceptable in the preview window.

6 Click **OK**.

What is image compression?

Image compression involves using mathematical techniques to reduce the amount of information required to describe an image. This results in small file sizes, which is important when transmitting information efficiently on the Web. Some compression schemes, such as JPEG, involve some loss in quality due to the compression, but the loss is usually negligible compared to the file size savings.

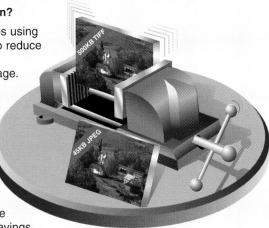

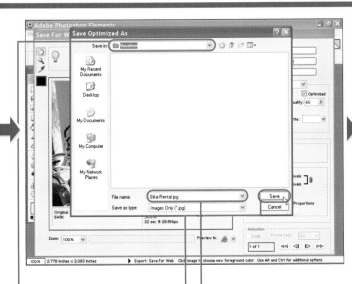

7 In Windows, click ⌄ and select a folder in which to save the file.

■ On a Mac, click ⬍ and then click the column view to locate a folder in which to save the file.

8 Type a filename.

■ Elements automatically assigns a .jpg extension.

9 Click **Save**.

■ Elements saves the JPEG file in the specified folder.

■ You can open the folder to access the file.

■ The original image file remains open in Elements.

SAVE A GIF FOR THE WEB

You can save a file as a GIF — Graphics Interchange Format — and publish it on the Web. The GIF format is good for saving illustrations that have a lot of solid color. The format supports a maximum of 256 colors.

SAVE A GIF FOR THE WEB

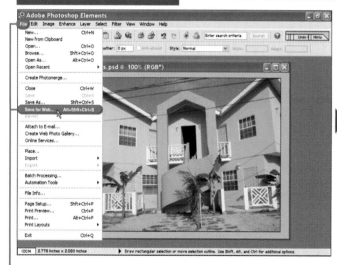

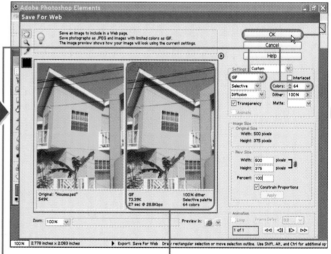

1 Click **File**.

2 Click **Save for Web**.

■ The Save For Web dialog box appears.

3 Click ⌄ (⬍) and select **GIF**.

4 Click ⬍ and select the number of colors to include in the image.

■ GIF allows a maximum of 256 colors, making it unsuitable for many photos.

5 Check that the file quality and size are acceptable in the preview window.

6 Click **OK**.

How do I minimize the file sizes of my GIF images?

The most important factor in creating small GIFs is limiting the number of colors in the final image. GIF files are limited to 256 colors or fewer. In images that have just a few solid colors, you can often reduce the total number of colors to 16 or 8 without any noticeable reduction in quality. See step **4** in this section for setting the number of colors in your GIF images.

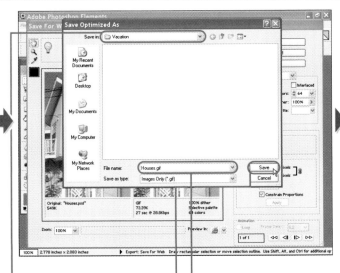

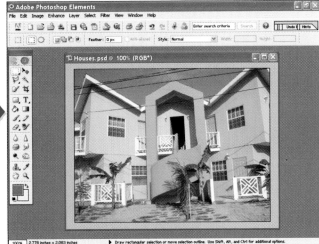

7 In Windows, click ⌄ and select a folder in which to save the file.

■ On a Mac, click ⬍ and then the column view to locate a folder in which to save the file.

8 Type a filename.

■ Elements automatically assigns a .gif extension.

9 Click **Save**.

■ Elements saves the GIF file in the specified folder.

■ You can open the folder to access the file.

■ The original image file remains open in Elements.

SAVE A GIF WITH TRANSPARENCY

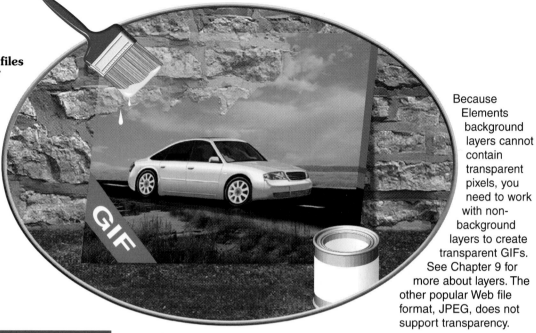

You can include transparency in files saved in the GIF file format. The transparent parts do not show up when you place the image on a Web page.

Because Elements background layers cannot contain transparent pixels, you need to work with non-background layers to create transparent GIFs. See Chapter 9 for more about layers. The other popular Web file format, JPEG, does not support transparency.

SAVE A GIF WITH TRANSPARENCY

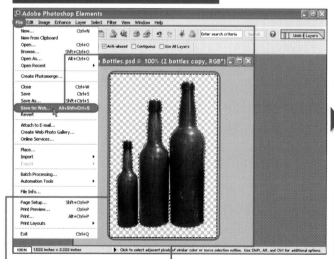

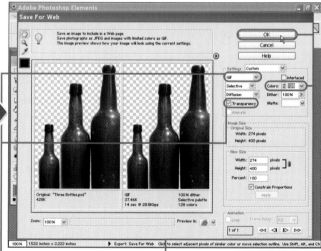

1 Select the area that you want to make transparent with a selection tool.

Note: See Chapter 4 to learn how to use the selection tools.

2 Press Delete to delete the pixels.

■ Elements replaces the deleted pixels with a checkerboard pattern.

3 Click **File**.

4 Click **Save for Web**.

5 Click ⌄ (⬍) and select **GIF**.

6 Click **Transparency** to retain transparency in the saved file (☐ changes to ☑).

7 Click ⬍ and select the number of colors to include in the image.

■ GIF allows a maximum of 256 colors.

8 Click **OK**.

What file size should I make my Web images?

If a large portion of your audience uses 56K modems to view your Web pages, keep your images small enough so that total page size — which includes all the images on the page plus the HTML file — is below 50K. You can check the file size and the download speed of an image at the bottom of the Save For Web preview pane. To change an image's file size and download speed, you can adjust the quality and color settings in the Save For Web dialog box. See the sections "Save a JPEG for the Web" and "Save a GIF for the Web" for details.

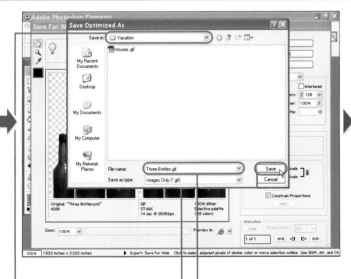

9 Click ⌄ and select a folder in which to save the file.

■ On a Mac, click ⬍ and then the column view to locate a folder in which to save the file.

10 Type a name for the file.

■ Elements automatically assigns a .gif extension.

11 Click **Save**.

■ In this example, the image has been added to a Web page and opened in a Web browser.

■ The transparency causes the Web page background to show through around the edges of the object.

SAVE A GIF WITH WEB-SAFE COLORS

You can save your GIF images using only Web-safe colors. This ensures that the images appear the way you expect in browsers running on 256-color monitors.

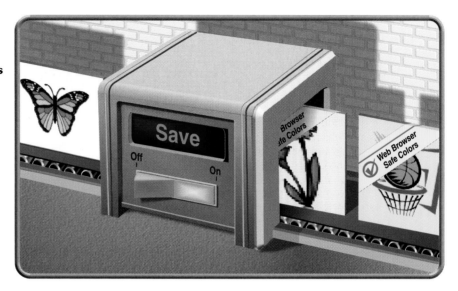

You can create Web-safe images only in the GIF format.

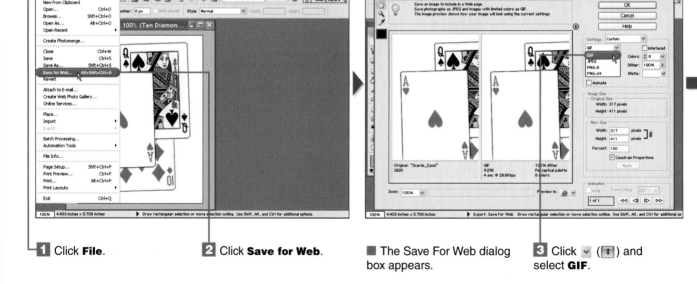

SAVE A GIF WITH WEB-SAFE COLORS

1 Click **File**.

2 Click **Save for Web**.

■ The Save For Web dialog box appears.

3 Click ⌄ (◆) and select **GIF**.

**Should I save all my Web images
with Web-safe colors?**

Not necessarily. Nowadays, most
people surf the Web on monitors
set to thousands of colors or
more, which makes Web safety
less relevant. Also, it is better to
save photographic Web images
as non-Web-safe JPEGs
because the GIF file format offers
poor compression and quality
when it comes to photos.

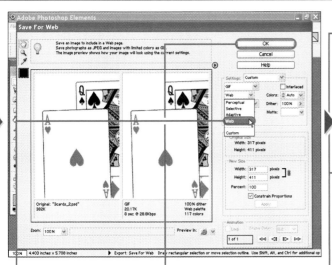

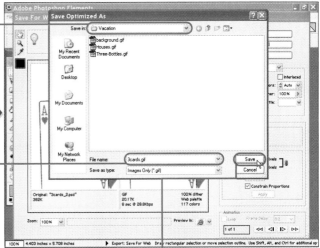

4 Click ∨ (⊡) and select
Web as the color palette
type.

*Note: When you do not specify Web-
safe colors, Elements saves the
image by choosing from all the
colors available in the spectrum.*

■ Elements now uses only
colors from the palette
available to browsers
running on 256-color
monitors.

5 Click **OK**.

6 Click ∨ and select a
folder in which to save the
file.

■ On a Mac, click ⊡ and
then click the column view to
locate a folder in which to
save the file.

7 Type a name for the file.

■ Elements automatically
assigns a .gif extension.

8 Click **Save**.

■ Elements saves the GIF
file in the specified folder.

■ You can open the folder to
access the file.

SAVE A GIF ANIMATION

You can create a multilayer Elements image and save it as an animated GIF file. Each layer serves as a frame in the animation. Frames are snapshots that show the animated object in different positions — like pages in a flip book. For more about layers, see Chapter 9.

You can view the animation in a Web browser.

SAVE A GIF ANIMATION

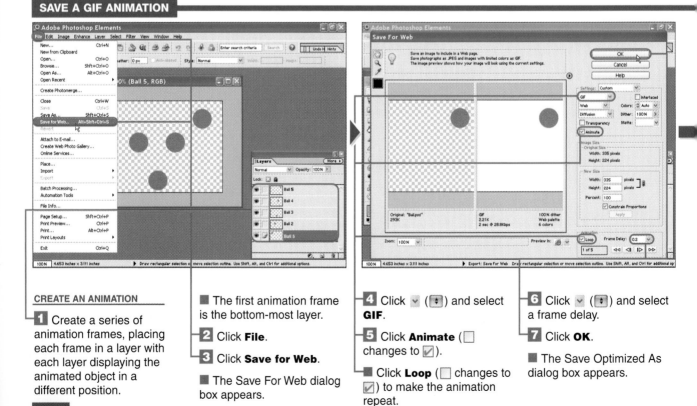

CREATE AN ANIMATION

1 Create a series of animation frames, placing each frame in a layer with each layer displaying the animated object in a different position.

■ The first animation frame is the bottom-most layer.

2 Click **File**.

3 Click **Save for Web**.

■ The Save For Web dialog box appears.

4 Click ⌄ (⬍) and select **GIF**.

5 Click **Animate** (☐ changes to ☑).

■ Click **Loop** (☐ changes to ☑) to make the animation repeat.

6 Click ⌄ (⬍) and select a frame delay.

7 Click **OK**.

■ The Save Optimized As dialog box appears.

How do I create GIF animations that display effectively?

- Because GIF images only display 256 colors, create them with flat-color art rather than photographs.

- Because frame speeds vary across systems, test your animations on a variety of platforms and browsers.

- Because multiple animation frames can quickly create large file sizes, check the file size in the Save For Web preview pane.

How do I use the animation controls to test my animated GIF?

You can use the control buttons in the Save for Web dialog box to move between animation frames.

◁◁	**Selects First Frame** ..... Displays the initial frame in your animation.
◁❙	**Selects Previous Frame** ... Moves to the previous frame in your animation.
❙▷	**Selects Next Frame** ..... Displays the next frame in your animation.
▷▷	**Selects Last Frame** ..... Displays the final frame in your animation.

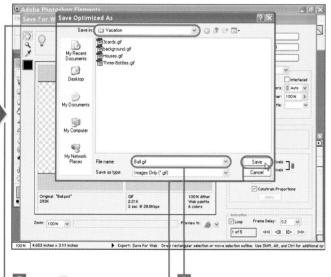

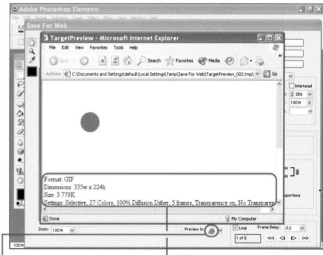

8 Click ☑ and select a folder in which to save the file.

■ On a Mac, click ⬆ and then click the column view to locate a folder in which to save the file.

9 Type a name for the file.

■ Elements automatically assigns a .gif extension.

10 Click **Save**.

■ Elements saves the animated GIF file.

PREVIEW THE ANIMATION

1 Repeat steps **1** through **6**.

2 In the Save for Web dialog box, click 🖼.

■ The GIF animation opens in a browser and plays.

■ General information about the image file displays below the image.

ADD CAPTION AND COPYRIGHT INFORMATION

You can store caption and copyright information with your saved image. You may find this useful if you plan on publishing the images online.

Some image editing applications — such as Elements — can detect copyright information from an image and display it to a user who opens it.

ADD CAPTION AND COPYRIGHT INFORMATION

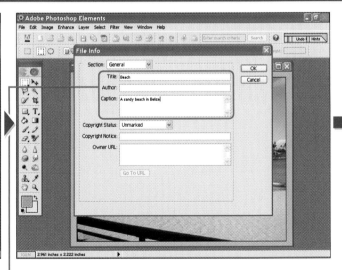

1 Click **File**.

2 Click **File Info**.

■ The File Info dialog box appears.

3 Type the caption and other information for your image.

■ With some printers, you can print the caption along with the image using settings in the Page Setup dialog box.

Note: See Chapter 15 for more on printing.

288

**How do I retrieve information
about a photo taken with a digital
camera?**

Information about photos taken
with a digital camera is stored as
EXIF information. You can view it
in the Caption dialog box by
clicking the Section ☑ (🔢) and
selecting **EXIF**. This information
includes the make and model of
the camera and the date and time
the photo was shot.

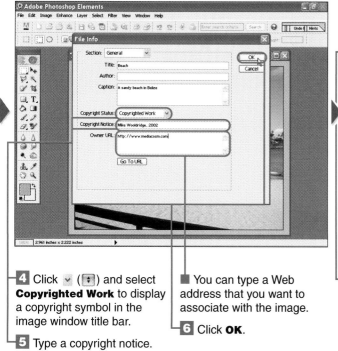

4 Click ☑ (🔢) and select
Copyrighted Work to display
a copyright symbol in the
image window title bar.

5 Type a copyright notice.

■ You can type a Web
address that you want to
associate with the image.

6 Click **OK**.

■ Elements places a
copyright symbol in the
title bar.

289

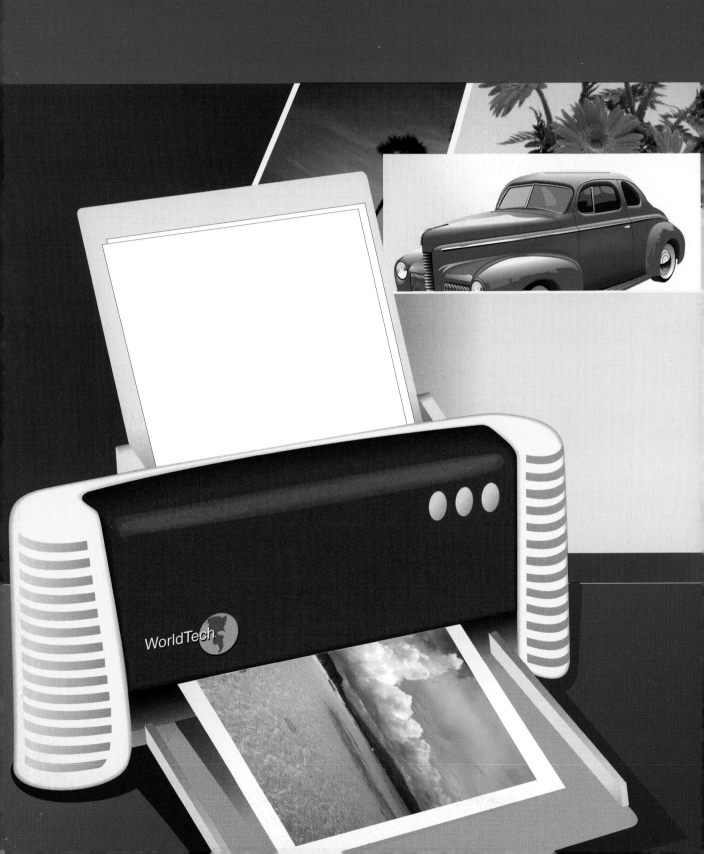

CHAPTER 15

Printing Images

Printing enables you to save the digital imagery you create in Photoshop Elements in hard-copy form. Elements can print to black-and-white or color printers.

PRINT AN IMAGE FROM A PC

You can print your
Photoshop Elements
image from a PC to
create a hard copy of
your work.

PRINT AN IMAGE FROM A PC

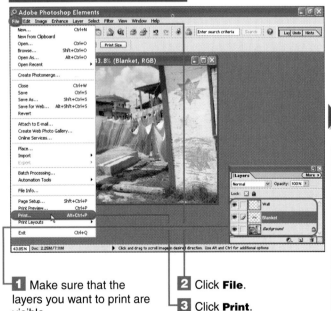

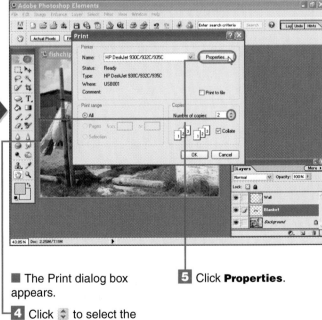

1 Make sure that the
layers you want to print are
visible.

*Note: An Eye icon ( ) means
that a layer is visible. To learn
more about layers, see Chapter 9.*

2 Click **File**.

3 Click **Print**.

■ The Print dialog box
appears.

4 Click ↕ to select the
number of copies.

5 Click **Properties**.

**What is the difference between
portrait and landscape
orientation?**

Portrait, which is the default
orientation for most printers, prints
with the long edge of the page
oriented vertically. A standard 8.5-
inch by 11-inch sheet of paper
measures 11 inches up and down
in portrait mode. Landscape prints
with the paper turned 90 degrees.
The long edge of the page is
oriented horizontally.

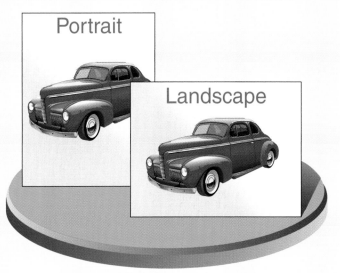

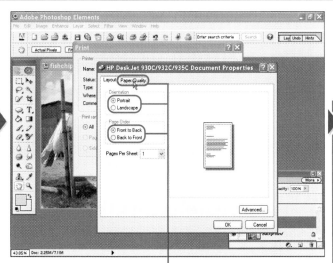

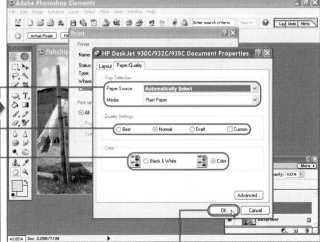

■ The Properties dialog
box appears.

*Note: The Properties dialog box
may vary depending on the printer
you have installed.*

6 Click an orientation
(○ changes to ⊙).

7 Click a page order
(○ changes to ⊙).

8 Click the **Paper/Quality**
tab.

9 Click a print quality
(○ changes to ⊙).

10 Click **Color** or **Black &
White** (○ changes to ⊙).

11 Select other properties
specific to your brand of
printer.

12 Click **OK**.

13 Click **OK** in the Print
dialog box.

■ The image prints.

PRINT AN IMAGE FROM A MAC

You can print your
Photoshop Elements
image from a Mac to
create a hard copy of
your work.

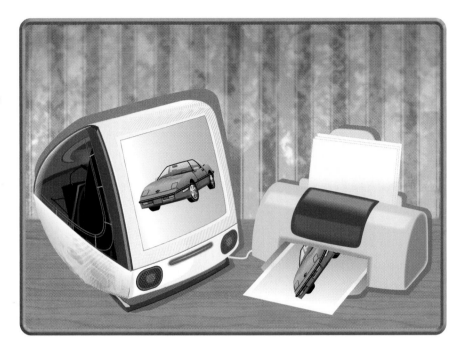

PRINT AN IMAGE FROM A MAC

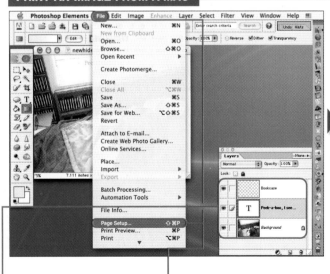

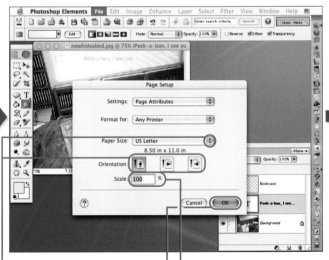

SET UP THE PAGE

1 Make sure that the
layers you want to print
are visible.

*Note: An 👁 means that a layer is
visible. To learn more about layers,
see Chapter 9.*

2 Click **File**.

3 Click **Page Setup**.

■ The Page Setup dialog
box appears.

4 Click ↕ and click a
paper type.

5 Click an orientation
button (🔲, 🔲, or 🔲).

■ You can type a value to
increase or decrease the
size of your image on the
page.

6 Click **OK**.

How do I print multiple pages on one sheet in Mac OS X?

The Layout option is especially useful in Elements because you can print 2 or 4 pages per sheet to create a greeting card layout. In the Print dialog box:

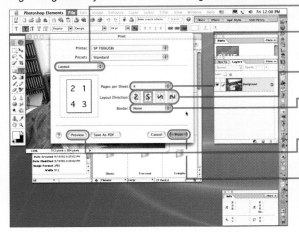

1 Click ▪ and click **Layout**.

2 Click ▪ and click the number of pages you want per sheet.

3 Click a layout direction option.

4 You can click here to select a border for your printout.

■ You can click **Preview** to preview your layout.

5 Click **Print**.

■ Elements prints multiple pages per your specifications.

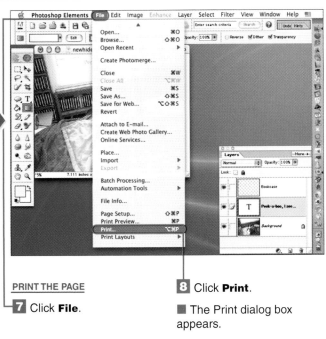

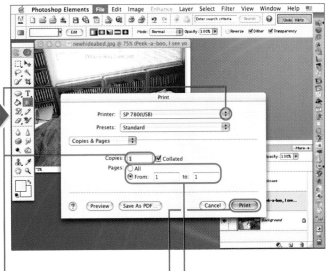

PRINT THE PAGE

7 Click **File**.

8 Click **Print**.

■ The Print dialog box appears.

9 Click ▪ and click a printer.

10 Type the number of copies you want.

11 Click a range of pages you want to print (○ changes to ●) and type a range, if necessary.

12 Click **Print**.

■ Your copies print.

Elements lets you preview your printout, as well as adjust the size and positioning of your printed image, in the Print Preview dialog box. Previewing lets you check your work without having to actually print on paper.

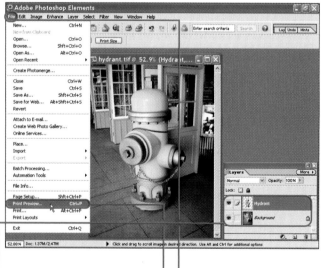

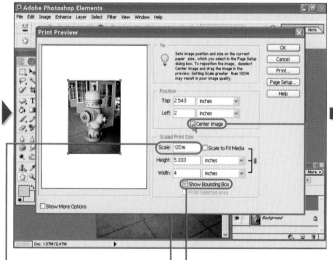

1 Make sure that the layers you want to print are visible.

Note: An 👁 means that a layer is visible. To learn more about layers, see Chapter 9.

2 Click **File**.

3 Click **Print Preview**.

■ The Print Preview dialog box appears.

4 Type a percentage in the Scale box to shrink or enlarge the image.

5 To reposition and resize the image, click **Show Bounding Box** (☐ changes to ☑).

6 Click **Center Image** to allow for the repositioning of the image (☑ changes to ☐).

**How can I maximize the size of
my image on the printed page?**

In the Print Preview dialog box,
you can click **Scale to Fit Media**
(☐ changes to ☑) to scale the
image to the maximum size for the
current printing settings.

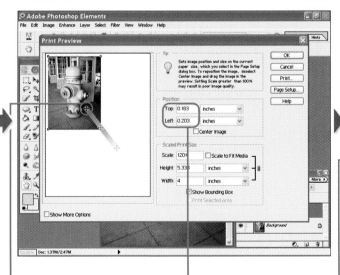

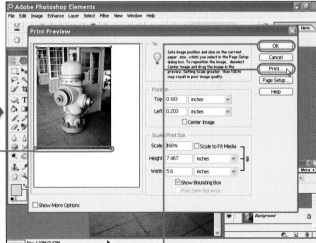

7 Click and drag in the
image window to reposition
the image on the page.

■ You can position your
image precisely by typing
values in the Top and Left
fields.

■ You can click and drag the
handles (☐) on the image
edges to scale the image.

8 Click **OK** to exit the Print
Preview dialog box.

■ To print the image, click
Print.

INDEX

convert
     color image to grayscale, 135
     color to grayscale, 140
     file types, 252–253
     image sizes, 254–255
     type of fill layer to another, 175
copy selections, 80–81
copyright information, 288–289
Create a New Image, 28–29
Crop an Image, 54–55
Crop tool, 52
Crystallize dialog box, 214
Crystallize filters, 214
cursor type setting, 17, 40
curved selections, Lasso tool, 60–61
custom brush, 103
custom pattern, define, 109
Custom Shape tool, 114–115, 116
custom shapes, accessing more, 117
customize Marquee tools, 59
Cutout filter, 226–227
cutout images, 226–227

D

darkening areas of images, 124
Default Colors, Red Eye Brush, 148
defaults
     file extensions, setting, 17
     measurement units, 17
     reset tool, 105
delete
     layers, 163
     selections, 82
     type, 239
digital cameras photo information, 289
digital photographs, 13, 23
dimensions
     canvas size, 53
     scale proportionally, 85
directional blurs, 207
Display & Cursors option, 17
Distort command, 210
Distort filters, 210–211
distort images, 210–211
distort selection, 87
dodge, 124

Dodge tool, 122, 124
dots painting, 103
draw
     lines, 116–117
     shapes, 114–115
drop shadows
     adding to image, 188–189
     adding to layers, 194–195
duplicate layers, 162
Dust & Scratches filter, 153
DV Stream files, 269

E

edge contrast, adjust with Magnetic Lasso tool, 63
effects
     application, 7
     Brushed Aluminum Frame effect, 191
     Lighting Effects filter, 222–223
     previewing, 193
     shadow effects, 189
Elements Toolbox
     Macintosh, 11
     PC, 10
Elliptical Marquee tool, 59
e-mail images, 266–267
emboss images, 224–225
emphasize objects, 126–127
enlarging palettes, 15
EPS (Encapsulated PostScript) files, 25, 275
equalize colors, 138–139
Equalize command, 138–139
erase flaws or elements, 146
Eraser tool, 94
EXIF information, 289
Exit Photoshop Elements, 31
Expand Selection dialog box, 72
Eye icon, 160
Eyedropper tool, 97
eyes, Red Eye Brush, 148–149

F

fancy backgrounds, add, 192–193
fancy covering to layers, add, 200–201
feather border selection, 90–91
Feather value, 59

INDEX

move selection
in background, 78
layer, 79
in straight line, 79
Move tool, 40, 78–79
mpeg file format, 269
mpg file format, 269
multimedia images resolution, 29

N

noise to images, 212–213

O

objects
de-emphasize, 126–127
remove from background, 64
Offset filter, 228
offset image, 228–229
on-screen image resolution, 29
on-screen size of images, 46–47
opacity
apply different, 109
brush decrease, 107
change layers, 166–167
Open an Image, 24–25
open images, 26–27
open palettes, 14
Options Bar
Macintosh, 11
PC, 10
organize photographs, 5
outer glow to layers, 198–199
outline type, 248
outlines, bold, 248
Output sliders, 129

P

Paint Bucket tool, 104–105
Paintbrush tool, 40, 94, 100–101
Palette Well
Macintosh, 11
PC, 10
palettes
close, 15
enlarge, 15
Macintosh, 11
open, 14
PC, 10

panoramic images, 262–265
paste selections, 80–81
pattern fill layers, 176–177, 177
Pattern Stamp tool, 108–109
PC
print document, 292–293
starting Photoshop Elements, 8
workspace, 10
PDF files, 25, 157, 276
PDF slideshows, 270–271
Pencil tool, 101
perspective, add to panorama, 265
Photocopy filter, 217
photographs
edit, 4
organizing, 5
Photomerge feature, 262–263
Photoshop Elements, exiting, 31
PICT files, 25
picture packages, 258–259
pictures, painting, 4
Pinch filter, 211
Pixelate filters, 214
pixels
choose, 6
image selections, 68
select, 64–65
PNG files, 275
Polygonal Lasso tool, 60–61
portrait orientation, 293
posterize colors, 139
Posterize command, 139
predefined set, brush styles, 102
preferences, set, 16–17
Preserve Transparency option, 111
preview
images printed size, 49
printouts, 296–297
print resolution of images, change, 50–51
print size
images, change, 48–49
versus on-screen size, 47
print
Macintosh, 294–295
PC, 292–293
printouts, preview, 296–297
PSD (Photoshop Document), 25
Pucker tool, 231

INDEX

W

Warp tool, 231
warp type, 246–247
Web files
    GIF, 280–281
    JPEG, 278–279
    size, 283
Web images, 13, 29
Web photo gallery, 260–261
Web-safe colors, 96, 284–285
width, adjust with Magnetic Lasso tool, 63
Width and Height boxes, 59
Wipe transitions, 271
workspace
    Macintosh, 11
    PC, 10

Z

Zoom tool, 6, 34–35, 40